eat nordic

The ultimate diet for
weight loss, health
and happiness

Trine Hahnemann
PHOTOGRAPHS BY LARS RANEK

QUADRILLE

What is the
Nordic diet?

The countries of the Northern Hemisphere have their own very healthy food culture, ingredients and traditions which have, for too long, been eclipsed by the perceived benefits of the cuisines of other nations deemed to be intrinsically better for us. Rediscovering our Northern heritage also helps us address several issues around food other than health.

Eating the Nordic way is grounded in tradition, but is also very much a modern everyday cuisine incorporating influences from other cultures. It is based on the produce available in the Northern hemisphere, where many grain and vegetable crops grow naturally or have ideal conditions for cultivation, where animals live wild or are farmed, and where fish that favour cold waters are caught.

THE FUNDAMENTALS OF THE NORDIC DIET

- Balanced meals with an emphasis on seasonal vegetables and whole grains.
- Home-cooking with fresh ingredients, including home-baked bread.
- Eat less.
- Eat fatty fish twice a week, like herring, mackerel and salmon.
- Eat vegetarian meals.
- Eat less poultry, game or meat.
- Take time to eat with friends and family on a daily basis.
- Exercise every day as part of your routine.

Scientific evidence supports the claim that a balanced diet based on a wide range of ingredients with a variety of minerals, vitamins, beneficial fatty acids and natural disease-fighting compounds will help you live a healthier and happier life. Of course, that alone is not enough. We also need to eat less; to exercise meal control. Over-eating is the biggest health problem we face. No quick diet really helps solve that, but a lifestyle change will. Balance is at the core of wellbeing.

The Nordic diet offers this balance, but it is allied with a growing organic, eco-conscious movement too and a focus on seasonality, so that during the year we try to dine more or less according to what nature has to offer. Coupled with that is an active outdoor lifestyle in which we cycle daily to work, and we take part in sport or other physical activities all year round. Whether we're hiking, skiing or swimming, nature is always part of our life even from infancy, when we spend time outside every day, no matter the weather.

The Nordic countries also offer a way of life that can add positively to the debate on the right balance between work, leisure, family time and time spent cooking and eating. In the Nordic countries we still cook a good deal and bake our own bread. The evening meal is still a daily family event and that is an important part of being happy and healthy. Cooking your own food gives you greater control over what you eat.

It is a myth that everything was better in the old days. The food industry was not as developed as it is now and, faced with various socio-economic problems, we were not capable of feeding the population after the Second World War. So when we consider all the problems today caused by the food industry, manifested in unrecognizable food that is full of additives, fat, sugar and salt, it becomes apparent that these are to some extent the result of circumstances in which we thought it necessary to produce food as efficiently and plentifully as possible. These developments were also linked to the fact that many more women had entered the workforce, and generally nobody else volunteered to take over the cooking. This created a huge gap for the food industry to fill and our food culture suffered immensely.

This is, of course, a very short and generalized description of a highly complex problem, because there are a lot of important issues at stake here. However, I believe that with the knowledge we have today about health, we have to move forward and stop romanticizing the past. We have to decide on the food culture we want in future and work out how we are going to get people back into their kitchens, to cook food themselves from fresh ingredients; and start baking again from nutritious wholegrain flour.

To eat Nordic is to cook food that is full of flavour, and to eat healthily without having to count calories or obey strict dietary rules. It affords us an opportunity to change our diet according to local produce, seasons, tradition and contemporary taste. Never before have the developed nations had access to so much food from all over the world; never has there been so much choice. However, in order to play our part in a sustainable global food culture, we must focus on our local cuisines, traditions and produce.

At this point in history we have an extraordinary opportunity to re-examine our food habits and, with our knowledge and technology, to develop a diet that encompasses different traditions with local produce.

Lifestyle
and Diet

Changing to a healthier lifestyle can be challenging, but the benefits are significant, so your efforts will pay off in the long run.

CHANGE YOUR DIET

Your aim is to cook and eat food that is really tasty and full of fresh flavours that will give you joy and make you feel fulfilled. This involves eating home-cooked meals where love and care have been put into their preparation. Set the table, sit down and enjoy the moment; eat slowly and get your palate to work.

Take care to eat three main meals a day made up of whole grains, vegetables and fruit, and

cut down on portion sizes. Your daily intake should be about 50-60% vegetables. In between meals you can snack on fruit and vegetables. Keep your blood sugar levels in balance and don't starve yourself, but don't eat if you are not hungry.

EXERCISE MORE AND SPEND
TIME OUTSIDE

No matter how healthily you eat, exercise is still a key to health and happiness. Your heart is a muscle and it needs to be exercised, so cardiovascular exercise is good for blood circulation, for stress levels and for general psychological wellbeing, as well as to maintain a steady weight throughout your life. If you don't exercise already, choose something you like - walking, swimming, running, cycling - something you will actually enjoy doing. Find other people to exercise with, set goals and make a bet as an incentive to continue.

We have a saying in Denmark: 'There is no such thing as bad weather, only wrong clothing'. We cycle a lot: to work, when shopping, and with our children. It's a great way to get around without being trapped in traffic. If you can't cycle to work, get off one stop before your destination and walk the rest

of the way. Take the stairs. Think about how to build regular exercise into your daily routine

ORGANIC AND LOCALLY SOURCED FOOD

I believe that organic food is better for your health than non-organically produced food, so eating organic is about what you believe is right. For me the main reason to eat this way is to ensure that we do not exploit the earth and that we maintain a holistic ecosystem. I do not like chemicals in my food – it's as simple as that.

I support buying locally, but I am also realistic. Living in a Nordic country in which food is not available locally all year round, we do need supplies from other regions. Wine, coffee, spices, lemons and tea are prime examples of things that I would really miss if I could only buy food produced up to 100 miles from where I live. So, for me, 'local' in many ways can just mean Europe. Like with most things, it's all about finding a balance.

EAT MEALS TOGETHER

Food must be a joy, not a burden or a chore, and this includes the social aspects of eating. I strongly believe it is immensely important to sit down regularly and eat together with other people. If I think about my dinner table, what comes to mind are all the meals I've shared with friends, eating well-prepared food, talking, laughing out loud, crying and enjoying all the stories told. It is also known

DEALING WITH CLIMATE CHANGE

We all have to do our bit to help reduce climate change and global warming. Most of our attention is focused on travel, especially air travel and cars and their exhausts, but the world's livestock production is responsible for a large part of all greenhouse gases. The calculation is clear: it takes ten times more energy to produce a steak from a corn-fed cow than to produce the oats needed for a portion of porridge.

The solution is not only to return to grass-fed cows but to cut back drastically on the amount of meat we eat. So the modification of your diet is an area in which you can make a difference immediately: stop eating meat every day; it's that simple. Cut down to a maximum of three times a week: your health will benefit and you will do your bit to alleviate climate change. When you do buy meat, spend more money on getting quality rather than on increasing the quantity.

One thing is sure: driving a car to buy groceries every day is not good for the planet. Retrain yourself to shop only a couple of times a week or less, and walk or cycle instead. But food transportation is also a complicated issue. We have established that for ecological and health concerns we need to cut down on meat consumption and eat more vegetables in our daily diet. The whole question of food mileage is very complicated, but I think one should be cautious about it: do your own research and make your own judgement.

SMALL STEPS TO FIGHT GLOBAL WARMING

- Reduce the amount of meat you eat.
- As much as possible, buy food that's in season.
- Choose locally grown fruit and vegetables that have not had to travel too far.
- Buy local fish, not exotic fish from the other side of the planet.
- Use your car as little as possible.

that countries where food is prepared from scratch and shared with other people have lower obesity rates.

Cooking healthy food from fresh ingredients, sitting down to share a meal: these are among the keys to healthy and happy living. I talk about this all the time, and the response I often get is: 'We don't have time, we work late.' Well, this is not necessarily true. You have plenty of time; you have a whole life full of time. Time is your capital; it is actually the most precious thing you have. The choice to be made is how to use that time. You have to ask: 'Do I want a healthy life that includes two of the most important things for my body – proper food and exercise?' Then plan it to be so, and make a conscious decision that home-cooked food and eating together are part of your life, and one thing you want to spend time doing.

The Ingredients
of the Nordic Diet

The Nordic diet is based around both the indigenous produce and what has grown well in the northern hemisphere through history: whole grains, root and green vegetables, fatty fish, poultry and wild game, berries and herbs – produce that will provide a super-healthy and balanced diet.

GRAINS

The grains used are those suited to cool climates – spelt, rye, oats and barley, all of which are high in fibre. But beware: these can be as refined and processed as most wheat flours, so it is vital to buy good-quality whole grains and wholegrain flours. Eat whole grains in salads, porridge or for dinner instead of potatoes or rice. Bake your own bread (see pages 154-173 for inspiration), or buy from

an artisan baker. Avoid mass-produced bread, which has little nutritive value and is full of additives to make it last.

VEGETABLES

Cabbages of all kinds – white, red, Savoy and pointed – together with their close relatives kale and Brussels sprouts, grow well in cold climates. They are full of flavour and can be cooked in many different ways.

Root vegetables are also important vegetables, especially in autumn and winter. They store well, and are versatile, filling and fuelling. Don't just stick with the usual potatoes and carrots: try beetroots, radishes, turnips, celeriac, parsnips, Hamburg parsley, Jerusalem artichokes, salsify and kohlrabi.

Green vegetables such as nettles, ramps (ramsons), Swiss chard, asparagus, peas, spinach, lettuce and leeks provide us throughout the spring and summer with a wide range of nutrients. Garlic and onion are also an important base of Nordic cooking all year round, both when it comes to flavour and nutrients.

Living in the wild, game meat is healthier, leaner and said by some to be more digestible. The best way to procure game is by knowing a local hunter. Game is very seasonal and the variety is greatest in autumn.

BERRIES

Blueberries and blackberries, red and blackcurrants, rose hips, cloudberries, lingonberries, gooseberries, strawberries and raspberries – some need to be grown commercially, while others are nature's gift to us, growing wild in the countryside, ripe for picking. In the cool Nordic countries with the long, light days and nights they get a lot of light but not a lot of warmth. So they grow slowly, and are small in size but big in taste.

They are very healthy due to their particularly high levels of antioxidants. The healthiest way to eat them is raw when in season, so take a walk in the woods, pick them fresh and eat them as soon as you can. Or as I do most of the time, buy them fresh when they have been picked within the past 24 hours.

HERBS

Herbs are so important in everyday cooking, adding flavour and freshness. Popular garden herbs include dill, parsley, chives, mint, tarragon, chervil, bay leaves, thyme and rosemary. But if you have access to wild herbs or can buy them from someone, the selection is enormous. I like to pick horseradish, elderflower, geranium and wood sorrel.

To get the most nutritional benefit from herbs, you have to eat large amounts, which you can do in soups, sauces, pestos or salads like tabbouleh. If you want to forage your own, get a guidebook and start exploring.

FISH AND SEAFOOD

Only eat locally caught fish. In the Nordic countries we eat especially oily fish like herring, salmon and mackerel, but we also have wonderful cod, lobster, haddock, mussels, oysters and lot of more rare local fish like garfish, different flatfish and a lot of wonderful fish roes.

MEAT, POULTRY AND GAME

The flavour in meat, poultry, and game comes from the animal's diet. Animals bred on pasture generally have a better flavour than meat from animals reared in pens or stalls.

Chicken and other poultry are a very important source of protein, and easy to prepare. However, a great deal of chicken today is not so much raised as manufactured. I always buy free-range or organic chicken – more expensive, but our whole philosophy should be one of quality first, and reducing how much and how often we eat it.

How to Lose Weight the Nordic Way

What is the right body weight? How should we look? These are very difficult questions to answer, but I believe it's most importantly about feeling comfortable in your own body. We are far too easily influenced by trends and public opinion. If you feel heavy, if your clothes are too tight and if you are tired, losing weight might be a good idea. But do it slowly and by changing your habits. There is no easy fix and crazy diets do not work.

Losing weight – and keeping it off – can be hard work because it involves life-changing decisions to find another way of eating and enjoying food. The rules couldn't be simpler, though: you need to eat less and exercise or be active. Being active improves your body's physical and mental state, so it is a win-win situation. However, getting into a routine is one of the most challenging aspects.

I have to emphasize that this is a general guideline. The metabolism varies from individual to individual, depending on age, gender, height, weight and your everyday activity levels. Furthermore, if you exercise regularly, the proportion of heavier muscular tissue to fat changes. New studies come out all the time demonstrating just how little we understand about why some people are heavier than others. Metabolism might be connected with our genes, or the bacteria in our stomachs. There is much we don't know.

The most crucial factor in weight loss, in my experience, is to change your lifestyle forever... and I mean forever. I can't recommend going on a diet for two to three weeks and then going back to eating like you used to. You can't expect to keep the pounds off; moreover such 'yo-yo' dieting can be very damaging to your health. Changing your lifestyle is key if you need to lose weight and maintain your new body weight. That means smaller portions and less food, more vegetables and complex carbs, less alcohol, fat and sugar – and some exercise every day.

It is really that simple and can be done without calculating anything. I don't mean you can't indulge ever again; I'm all for having fun, wonderful food and nice wine. I am talking about changing your habits and your palate, so you end up preferring real-tasting food that is good for you.

GROUND RULES BEFORE STARTING A DIET
Before you start your diet, take the decision to make these changes a permanent feature of your life from now on. After some months without a lot of the things you were used to, such as crisps, chips, fizzy drinks, sugar in everything, heavy sauces, etc., they will actually lose their appeal... I promise. Real flavours from real food can truly change your preferences!

Take time to plan and cook: eating on the move is not a good solution, and shopping for food when you are very hungry and your blood sugar levels are low is also a bad idea. Therefore, plan for three to four days ahead or maybe even for a whole week.

Eating together at a set table is important – don't eat in front of the TV!

Make sure your dinner plates are not too big; using smaller plates is a good way to control portion sizes.

Eat all your meals slowly, enjoy your food and taste it. I mean really taste it and focus on what's on your plate. Learning to eat slowly can be hard in the beginning; I know from my own experience. At the beginning I put my watch next to the plate to keep track of time, and promised myself that the eating had to take at least 30 minutes. It took me a couple of months to get into the habit. I lose the habit frequently and then I have to go back to timing my meals.

Involve other people for support. If you find it difficult to change your habits, tell them how they can help you to achieve your goals.

SLEEP
Make sure you get enough sleep. Sleep deprivation makes you eat more since it will make you suffer from tired spells during the day and then you will be inclined to turn to sugar as the solution.

PLANNING YOUR WEIGHT-LOSS DIET
Start your new diet by examining everything in your cupboards, getting rid of not-very-healthy convenience items, such as ready meals, canned soups, snack bars, milk chocolate,

BMI = weight in kilograms [divided by] (height in meters)^2 [squared]

BMI	STATUS
Below 18.4	Underweight
18.5-24.9	Normal
25-29.9	Overweight
30 and above	Obese

fizzy drinks, crisps, cereals containing sugar, etc. Then restock your cupboards with real food, spices, good oils and vinegars, whole grains, oats, nuts, flours, mustards. This replacement process can, of course, be rather expensive. If so, you can do it over time, but try to get rid of all the unhealthy choices in your cupboards as quickly as possible. That is the surest way not to be tempted to eat them.

Plan what to eat for the whole week ahead, and then only go shopping twice so that you spend time in the kitchen instead of in the shops. When on a diet, planning is the key to success. Shopping when hungry or on the spur of the moment will almost inevitably mean that the wrong things get in your basket.

Make sure you always have vegetables, fresh and dried fruit and nuts in the house, so when you get really hungry or fatigued you have something safe to eat.

Lunch

In a busy working life you often have to buy lunch or go out for lunch as part of your job. When going out for lunch, do not eat bread and try to avoid alcohol. If it ends up being a big lunch, skip dinner or just eat a raw carrot. Being a little bit hungry now and then will not hurt you.

If you have to buy a takeaway lunch, always avoid sandwiches and go for salad, preferably one with whole grains or quinoa. In any case, the main rule is to stay away from factory-made bread.

High days and holidays

Holidays are always exceptions, and it is only natural to gain a little weight after a couple of weeks with good food and wine every day. That is OK and part of life, but make sure you exercise and perhaps increase your activity level while you have time on your hands.

If you go to a party or have a day when you lunch with friends, or any event where you eat more than planned, just cut down on the following days and you will still lose the amount you need for that week. Dieting is a process that cannot be evaluated day by day but only over weeks or months.

Salt

Sodium is an essential mineral, which we mostly get from salt. Unfortunately, getting too much salt is linked with risk of high blood pressure and heart disease. Your average intake should not be higher than 6g per day. Weigh 6g salt and see how much it is – that will give you a clear picture of the exact amount and help you to limit it. To avoid too much salt in your diet, do not eat processed food, takeaways, and lots of biscuits and snack bars; they contain a lot of salt because it is a natural flavour enhancer.

Sugar

Over the last few decades sugar has become the big enemy, not because there is anything wrong with it as such – it is gastronomically a fantastic ingredient and I would not live without it. However, consuming sugar in the quantities we do is a real and threatening problem, leading to all sorts of health issues.

Stop using sugar in your tea and coffee, but do not replace it with any sweetener. Instead get used to the true taste of the coffee and tea. Do this in stages if necessary. Stop drinking fizzy drinks on a daily basis, and instead buy or make some organic cordials (see page 153) and dilute them with water. Stop eating snack bars, chocolate bars, bought cakes and biscuits, and sweets. When craving sweet things, bake yourself a cake so you control exactly what goes into it, that is, the quantity of sugar and the quality of the other ingredients. Alternatively, eat fruit instead. Even though it also contains sugar, it is still a healthy option.

WHAT SHOULD YOU AIM FOR?

If you want to lose weight in a healthy and steady way, I recommend losing 1-2 pounds (500g-1kg) per week, no more. That way you will not feel starved or exhausted. The weight loss will all be due to change. Be patient if nothing really happens in the beginning; just stick to it and the weight will start coming off.

When you have to lose weight, it is important to maintain a steady blood sugar level. You do that by eating three main meals a day and three snacks, but the rule is: do not eat if you are not hungry. The diet plan opposite will work if you do not sit still all day but move around 20% of the time, and exercise two to three times a week.

SUGGESTED DIET PLAN

Breakfast
• 1 portion of raw oats with fruit and non-fat skimmed milk, or porridge, or a piece of rye bread with cottage cheese (see the recipes on pages 24-35).
• Coffee or tea* (with no sugar).

Morning snack
• 1 piece of rye bread with 2 tablespoons of low-fat cottage cheese, or if at a desk far away from a kitchen, have some raw vegetables and 10g nuts, like walnuts, hazelnuts or almonds.

Lunch
• A standard lunch with pieces of 1 slice of rye bread with hard-boiled eggs or potatoes, and a portion of raw vegetables like carrots, cauliflower, cucumber and celery sticks. At weekends or at home, when you have more time and a kitchen is available, make a soup or some of the other lunch recipes in the book.

Afternoon snack
• 1 piece of fruit.

Dinner
• 1 piece of fish, poultry or game, about 100-150g (except for days where the meal is vegetarian).
• 1 big portion of vegetables.
• 2 potatoes or 50g boiled grains.
• 1 portion of salad, with lettuce, kale or cabbage.

Choose from the recipes in the book.
Divide each week as follows:
3 days with vegetarian meals
2 days with fish
2 days with poultry, game or meat.

When having your main meal, make sure you set the table nicely, prepare your food with love, take time eating at the table with your family or friends. If eating alone, still set the table and serve yourself a wonderful tasty dinner.

Eat only one portion of food, then eat slowly and drink plenty of water while eating. That also prolongs the meal.

Always serve a fresh salad according to the season; fresh raw vegetables fill you up and they are super healthy. When on a diet, avoid dressings; instead use lemon juice or a nicely flavoured, good-quality vinegar instead.

In general, cut down on fat. Steam or bake instead of frying.

Evening snack
100ml non-fat yoghurt or skyr with berries or other seasonal fruit or, some nights, a small piece of dark chocolate.

General
Drink 2 litres of water a day, and always have raw vegetables in a plastic bag to snack on if hungry or getting sugar cravings.

*Coffee and tea are unlimited, but be careful not to have too much caffeine, which can make you giddy, especially if you do not eat a lot. Always use skimmed milk in your coffee and tea. Avoid café latte – there's too much fat in all that milk, and that goes for soy latte as well.

breakfast

Breakfast is a very important meal. A healthy, balanced breakfast with a good content of complex carbohydrates gives you a better start to the day, particularly in the case of children. It is therefore crucial not to make it a meal of white bread or sugary cereals, because these will not give you sufficient energy to see you through the morning. Instead, have something hearty, like whole grains, fruit, vegetables and eggs, which will keep hunger at bay at least until lunchtime. And on the weekend, make it into a feast and take your time over it.

Juices

A juice is a great start to the day. If you really want to lose weight, then devoting one day a week to consuming only juice helps you to eat less and exercise meal control. It is also a helpful way to keep your weight stable. Juices can be a combination of almost all vegetables and fruit, herbs and spices. Here are just three of my favourites. ALL SERVE 2.

Super green

700g cucumber
1 lime
400g apple (or alternatively, pineapple)
4-6 sprigs of tarragon

Wash the cucumber, cut away the green peel and white pith of the lime, and, if using pineapple, core it and cut away the peel of. Put the cucumber, lime flesh, apple or pineapple and tarragon in a juicer and juice until smooth. Serve right away or keep cold in the refrigerator.

My favourite red

500g beetroot
700g carrot
20g fresh turmeric
2 celery sticks

Peel the beetroot, carrot and turmeric. Put the beetroot, carrot, turmeric and celery in a juicer and juice until smooth. Serve right away or keep cold in the refrigerator.

Popeye's energy drink

500g spinach
400g Galia melon
1 lemon

Rinse the spinach in cold water, cut away the peel of the melon and deseed it, then cut the flesh into chunks, and cut away the yellow peel and white pith of the lemon. Put the spinach, melon and lemon flesh in a juicer and juice until smooth. Serve right away or keep cold in the refrigerator.

Smoothies

These make super-fast and great breakfasts. All sorts of smoothies can be made easily, you just need a blender, frozen or fresh fruit, fruit juice or low-fat yoghurt and some honey, then mix these any way you like to create your favourite smoothie. ALL SERVE 2.

Redcurrant smoothie

300g fresh or frozen
    redcurrants
1 banana, peeled
100ml redcurrant cordial
300ml low-fat yoghurt
honey, to sweeten (optional)
handful of ice cubes
    (if using fresh fruit)

Place all the ingredients in a blender and blend. Taste and sweeten with honey if you like. Serve right away in tall glasses.

Blueberry smoothie

300g blueberries
100ml apple juice
1 banana, peeled
300ml low-fat yoghurt
10 ice cubes
honey, to sweeten (optional)

Place all the ingredients in a blender and blend. Taste and adjust the sweetness with some honey if you like. Serve right away in tall glasses.

Strawberry and raspberry smoothie

300g fresh or frozen
    strawberries and
    raspberries
1 banana, peeled
100ml orange juice
500ml low-fat yoghurt
honey, to sweeten (optional)
handful of ice cubes
    (if using fresh fruit)

Place all the ingredients in a blender and blend. Taste and sweeten with honey if you like. Serve right away in tall glasses.

BERRIES of all types contain large amounts of antioxidant vitamins A and C. They are also sweet, sour and lovely to eat year round - either fresh in summer or frozen in smoothies in winter, for example.

Raw oats with fruit
and milk in summer

60g raw rolled oats
50g redcurrants
6 raspberries
200ml skimmed milk

SERVES 1

TIP The rolled oats can be replaced
with 2 WeetaBix.

VARIATION For a winter version
of this, you can replace the berries
with 50g diced apple and 20g
seedless raisins.

This was my childhood breakfast, and I still eat this most
mornings. Sometimes I mix in rye and spelt flakes, so that
it is not just oats. I always eat organic flakes with skimmed
milk and then whatever fruit I have in the house.

Add the oats to a serving bowl as a little mountain in the
middle. Place the fruit around the oats, pour the milk over
everything and eat right away.

Øllebrød (Rye and beer porridge)

300g rye bread,
  preferably stale
800ml water
1 tsp grated unwaxed
  lemon zest
2-3 tbsp lemon juice
200ml light Pilsner or
  alcohol-free beer
100g brown sugar
cold skimmed milk, to serve

SERVES 2-3

TIP If you serve this as a dessert,
accompany it with whipped cream.

One of my favourite types of porridge, I had this for both breakfast and dinner when I was a child and my parents were students on a budget. This is true comfort food and whenever I make it, I am instantly transported back to my childhood.

The day before, place the bread in a bowl, cover with the 800ml water, and leave overnight.

The next day, place the contents of the bowl in a pan and slowly bring to the boil. Stir well, add the lemon zest, beer and sugar, boil, and keep stirring for 5 minutes.

Serve warm with cold skimmed milk.

Spelt pancakes
with blueberries

2 eggs
400ml buttermilk
1 vanilla pod
200g wholegrain
   stoneground spelt flour
100g plain flour
1 tsp baking powder
½ tsp bicarbonate of soda
1½ tsp coarse sea salt
300g fresh blueberries
75g butter, for frying
runny honey or syrup,
   to serve

SERVES 4 (12 PANCAKES)

TIP If you want to lose weight, eat
one pancake with 100g fruit as your
weekend treat, but don't add any
honey or syrup.

**Spelt has a lovely sweet taste which works really well
with breakfast pancakes. The benefit of using spelt is
that you get more fibre, because it's a wholegrain flour
and therefore you're consuming slow carbs.**

To make the pancake batter, beat the eggs together in a
large mixing bowl. Add the buttermilk and beat again. Split
the vanilla pod lengthwise and scrape out the seeds with the
tip of a knife. Mix the vanilla seeds, flours, bicarbonate of soda
and salt together, then add to the egg mixture and beat again
until smooth. Mix in 125g of the blueberries.

Melt a little butter in a frying pan and, using a soup spoon,
place 3 separate spoonfuls in the pan so that you fry 3 small
round pancakes at a time, turning them gently once, until
nicely browned on both sides. Keep each batch warm under
a tea towel while you cook the rest.

Serve right away, topped with more fresh blueberries and
honey or syrup.

Smørrebrød
(open sandwiches
on rye bread)

These easy and healthy breakfast ideas also make perfect snacks at any time during the day. If you are aiming to lose weight, it is very important to eat small meals during the day so that your blood sugar levels do not drop drastically, causing you to go for a high-sugar quick fix like a chocolate bar. In the strawberry season, the perfect afternoon snack is a strawberry 'madder', a piece of rye bread with a very simple topping. BOTH SERVE 2.

Rye bread with strawberries

200g strawberries
2 slices of rye bread

Cut the strawberries in half, then place them on rye bread and eat right away.

VARIATION Mash some raspberries gently and spread out evenly on a piece of rye bread like jam, and you have the perfect summer 'mad'.

Rye bread, cottage cheese, herbs and vegetables

200g cottage cheese
2 tbsp chopped chives
2 tomatoes, deseeded and cut into
    small dice
⅓ cucumber, halved, deseeded and
    cut into small dice
salt flakes and freshly ground pepper
2 slices of rye bread

Place the cottage cheese in a bowl and mix with the other ingredients except the seasoning and the bread. Season to taste with salt and pepper. Place on top of the slices of rye bread and serve right away.

Eggs on rye toast
with spinach

1kg fresh spinach
salt and freshly ground
   pepper
4 slices of rye bread
8 organic eggs
50ml skimmed milk
1 tbsp rapeseed oil
10 wild garlic leaves, or
   chives or spring onion
   greens, chopped
10 cherry tomatoes, diced

SERVES 4

During weekends, when we have enough time to enjoy a long breakfast, I cook a meal that is more time-consuming and eat it with my husband while we relax and enjoy reading the newspapers. Eggs are a real treat, they are easy to digest and they give a fantastic boost to start your metabolism in the morning.

Start by preparing the spinach: remove any tough stems from the leaves and rinse 3 or 4 times in cold water. Drain in a colander.

Wilt the spinach in a sauté pan for 3 minutes. Season with salt and pepper, then drain in a colander again.

Put the bread to toast.

Mix the eggs in a bowl, beat them for 1 minute, then beat in the milk. Season the mixture. Add the oil to the sauté pan, heat gently then pour the egg mixture into the pan. Add the leaves, chives or greens, lower the heat, and cook gently. Just before the eggs start to set, add the tomatoes.

Place a slice of rye toast on each plate, divide the spinach between them, then add the eggs, sprinkle with pepper and serve right away.

Soft-boiled egg with toasted rye bread and smoked salmon

2 large organic eggs
2 slices of rye bread
4 slices of smoked salmon
a little handful of watercress

to serve
coarse sea salt and freshly
    ground black pepper

SERVES 2

Boiling eggs is a mystery. It takes training and concentration, and it is unbelievable that something so simple goes wrong so frequently. Often – and therefore most likely – we don't know how old our eggs are, and fresh eggs take a bit longer to cook than those that are a week old. The size of the eggs also matters. All in all, if you are a newcomer to the art of boiling eggs, just practise and you will learn eventually.

Place the eggs in a small pan with just enough cold water to cover. Bring to the boil, lower the heat and let it simmer gently for 3 minutes.

While the eggs are cooking, toast the rye bread and place the salmon on a small plate. Place the watercress on top of that and sprinkle with pepper. When the eggs are cooked, rinse them under cold running water. Drain and place them in egg cups.

Serve with the smoked salmon and rye bread on the side.

light lunches

Ensuring you get a healthy lunch can be a challenge, because we often rely on what other people have cooked for us, or on what we can buy. In Copenhagen, I run a canteen business called Hahnemanns Køkken where we serve lunch for 3,000 people every day – all home-cooked with good ingredients. So I know how vital lunch is. If you don't have a proper canteen, your lunch needs planning, either with regard to buying lunch or taking the time to make lunch in advance. Bring a small army of raw vegetables, left over from your dinner, or a sandwich on healthy bread like rye bread. If you buy grab-and-go dishes, focus on salads, as soups are often very rich and contain too much salt. Check the label or ask about the ingredients. I know what you are thinking: 'I don't have time for that!' But if you do not have time to take care of yourself and your health, you need to start to make changes.

Baked fish and parsley pesto sandwich

400g skinless fish fillets
salt and freshly ground
    pepper
2 spelt or rye buns
100g fresh salad leaves
2 tomatoes, sliced

parsley pesto
1 large bunch of parsley
30g almonds (with
    their skins)
1 small garlic clove, chopped
3 tbsp freshly grated
    Parmesan cheese
3 tbsp grapeseed oil
juice from 1 lemon
salt and freshly ground
    pepper

SERVES 2

TIP Save the rest of the pesto for
a salad, or serve it with a piece of
grilled fish or chicken breast.

**This is just a simple but good sandwich for lunch. The
shower bun dough (page 161) is very suitable to make
into big flat sandwich bread for this sandwich. Parsley is
a rather overlooked healthy food, rich in lots of nutrients.**

Preheat the oven to 200ºC/gas mark 6.

Start by making the pesto: put all the ingredients except
the lemon juice, salt and pepper in a blender, and blend to a
smooth paste. Season to taste with lemon juice, and some salt
and pepper.

Place the fish fillets in an ovenproof dish, sprinkle with salt
and pepper and bake in the oven for 10 minutes.

Cut the buns in half and spread some pesto on both halves
of each, then place some salad on that, then the baked fish
and then the tomatoes.

Serve with the fish either warm or cold.

Stinging nettle soup

1 yellow onion
1 tbsp olive oil
1.3 litres organic vegetable
   bouillon
¼ tsp ground nutmeg
200g stinging nettles
   (see recipe introduction)
salt and freshly ground
   pepper
a few sprigs of watercress,
   to serve
4 organic eggs, to serve

garlic croutons
2 slices of rye or spelt
   bread, cut into cubes
1 tbsp olive oil
1 garlic clove, finely
   chopped
salt and freshly ground
   pepper

SERVES 4

Stinging nettle soup should be made in May, when the stinging nettle has a lot of top leaves. Pick only the 4 or 5 top shoots. Nettle leaves are also good in scrambled eggs and frittatas – just blanch the leaves before use.

First make the croutons: preheat the oven to 180°C/gas mark 4. Mix the bread cubes with the oil and garlic, salt and pepper, and bake in the oven for 10 minutes.

In a large pan, sauté the onion in the oil for 5 minutes without allowing it to burn or colour too much. Add the vegetable bouillon and nutmeg, bring to the boil and add the nettle leaves. Leave to simmer for 20 minutes.

Using a hand blender, blend the soup, then season with salt and pepper.

Bring some water to the boil in a small pan. When the water is boiling, place the eggs in the water, turn down the heat and let simmer for 7 minutes, remove from the heat and place under cold water for 30 seconds. Take out and shell right away.

Serve the soup with the boiled eggs cut across in half and the croutons and watercress scattered on top.

STINGING NETTLES are an old medicinal herb and their stems have been used for weaving textiles since at least the Bronze Age. It grows everywhere in the countryside where the soil contains a certain level of nitrogen. Cooking or drying completely neutralizes the plant's toxic components. It must be picked in spring and early summer before flowering.

Cold cucumber soup

600g cucumbers
1 Galia melon, about 400g
500ml yoghurt
2 tbsp chopped mint
juice of 2 limes
50g watercress
salt and freshly ground
   pepper

to serve
watercress
Spelt Bread (page 171)

SERVES 4

On a very hot summer's day, when you don't really have a big appetite, serve this clear, fresh, tasty soup.

Peel the cucumbers and then halve, deseed and dice them; you should end up with about 500g. Peel the melon, deseed it and cut it into cubes. Put all the ingredients in a blender and blend until smooth. Season to taste with salt and pepper.
   Serve cold, garnished with watercress and alongside some spelt bread.

Mussel soup with potatoes and leeks

1kg mussels
1 tbsp rapeseed oil
1 onion, finely chopped
2 garlic cloves, chopped
3 leeks, cut into slices
1 tbsp tarragon leaves
salt and freshly ground
    pepper
4 large potatoes, peeled
    and diced
Country Bread (page 168),
    to serve

SERVES 4

New England clam chowder is a wonderful tasting soup. Here is my Nordic version, which has a great flavour and a lighter texture.

Scrub the mussels thoroughly and tug out any beards that may be hanging from the shells. Discard broken or open mussels or those that refuse to close when tapped. Rinse the mussels in water a couple of times.

Heat the oil in a big saucepan. Add the onion, garlic and leeks, and cook for 3 minutes. Add the mussels with the tarragon, 1 litre of water, and salt and pepper. Bring to a simmer and let simmer for 15 minutes.

Take out the mussels with a slotted spoon. Remove the mussels from the shells and discard the shells. Take out 200ml of the soup and place in another saucepan. Add 2 of the diced potatoes to that and let it simmer for 15 minutes.

To the large pot with the soup add the shelled mussels with the juice and the leeks etc. that came out with mussels. Add the rest of the potatoes and let simmer for 15 minutes.

Blend the potato soup in the small pan with a hand blender until it is a smooth, heavy soup, then add it back to the main soup and heat it up. Season to taste with salt and pepper.

Serve the soup very hot with Trine's Country Bread.

Leek soup with rye croutons

2 tbsp olive oil
2 shallots, diced
3 garlic cloves, chopped
2 tsp ground cardamom
1 tbsp ground coriander
500g leeks, well rinsed
   and cut into slices
3 bay leaves
1.5 litre organic vegetable
   bouillon
salt and freshly ground
   pepper

to serve
4 slices of rye or spelt
   bread, cut into cubes,
   to serve
20g butter

SERVES 4

TIP This is a very easy vegetable
soup, and can be used with different
vegetables; if you add potatoes
and root vegetables, use 1kg peeled
weight and then blend it when
cooked and season to taste.

This nourishing soup is easy to make and very inexpensive.
I believe that eating vegetable soup for the evening meal
once a week is a good way to organize your diet, giving you
a day without meat, a day where you save money and a day
when your supper is healthy and fibre-intensive.

Add the oil to a large pot, then add the shallot, garlic,
cardamom and coriander, and cook gently for 2-3 minutes.
Stir in the leeks and bay leaves. Add the bouillon and bring
to the boil. Turn down the heat and let simmer for 10 minutes.
Season to taste with salt and freshly ground pepper.
   Toast the bread cubes in a pan with the butter until golden
brown, tossing them frequently and being careful not to let
them burn.
   Serve the soup very hot, scattered with the croutons.

Cauliflower soup spiced with green chilli and served with prawns

1 large cauliflower
1 green chilli, deseeded
    and chopped
5 spring onions, chopped
2 baking potatoes, peeled
    and cut into cubes
2 tsp salt and freshly ground
    pepper

to serve
400g shelled, cooked,
    extra-large cold-water
    prawns
watercress
spelt bread

SERVES 4

TIP This soup can also be made
with broccoli.

People either love cauliflower or can't stand its funny, earthy taste. I love it and eat it raw, in a soup or in curries. My grandmother would boil it for a long time, then serve it whole with shrimps around it and a white sauce on the side. This is my modern version of that recipe.

Cut the cauliflower with the stalk into large pieces. Place all the ingredients in a large saucepan with 1.5 litres of water. Cover with a lid and bring to the boil. Reduce the heat and let it simmer for 20 minutes.

With a hand blender, blend to a smooth soup and then reheat. Season to taste with salt and pepper.

Arrange the prawns on 4 wooden skewers and serve them on top of the soup. Garnish with watercress sprigs and serve with spelt bread.

Smørrebrød with salmon tartare

400g very fresh salmon
  fillet, skinned
2 cucumbers, halved and
  deseeded
2 tbsp grated fresh
  horseradish
juice of 1 lime
1 tsp white wine vinegar
6 tbsp chopped chervil,
  plus 4 sprigs to decorate
salt and freshly ground
  pepper
4 slices of rye bread
8 crisp lettuce leaves

SERVES 4

In Denmark smørrebrød (open sandwiches) are eaten by lots of people every day for lunch – the permutations of healthy rye bread topped with fresh ingredients are endless. Nordic salmon, both marinated and cured, is world-famous, but serving it raw with horseradish is a great combination. For this treatment it is essential that you have a good supplier to ensure the salmon is very fresh. Please buy salmon that is MSC certified.

Cut the salmon fillet into small squares and place in a bowl. Cut the cucumbers into cubes. Add to the salmon with the horseradish, lime juice, vinegar and chopped chervil. Mix well and season with salt and pepper.

Place a slice of bread on each plate, place 2 lettuce leaves on each slice of bread, then spoon the salmon salad onto the lettuce leaves. Sprinkle with pepper and top with a sprig of chervil.

Smørrebrød for autumn and winter

Smørrebrød can be almost anything on bread; it is about getting the texture and flavours right. If you want to bring a rye bread sandwich to work, keep all the ingredients in small, separate containers and assemble just before eating. Smørrebrød is a perfect way to use up your leftovers. ALL SERVE 2.

Roast beef

2 Portobello mushrooms, chopped
1 tsp butter
2 slices of rye bread
4 slices roast beef
freshly ground pepper

pickled carrot
100ml apple cider vinegar
40g sugar
2 cloves
½ tsp coriander seeds
1 carrot, shaved into ribbons
1 spring onion, thinly sliced

Whisk together the vinegar, sugar and spices, then add the carrot and spring onion and leave for 30 minutes.
　Fry the mushrooms in the butter and season with salt and pepper. Top the rye bread with the beef, mushrooms and pickles. (The brine can be saved and used again). Season with pepper.

Cauliflower with sweet and sour topping

3 slices of rye bread
100g cauliflower

topping
3-4 tbsp cress
1 tbsp capers
1 tbsp diced red onion
1 tsp honey
1 tbsp extra virgin olive oil
2 tsp white wine vinegar
1 tbsp Dijon mustard
freshly ground pepper

Steam the cauliflower until al dente, then cool and chop.
　Mix all the ingredients for the topping. Crumble one of the slices of rye bread into crumbs and toast in a dry pan. Top the remaining slices of bread with the cauliflower, then the topping, some breadcrumbs, and the cress.

Smoked salmon

2 slices of rye bread
4 slices of smoked salmon
freshly ground pepper

topping
1 plum
50g red cabbage, shredded
1 tbsp balsamic vinegar
2 tbsp grated horseradish

Take the stone out of the plum and cut the flesh into small slices. Mix with the cabbage and vinegar.
　Top the rye bread with the salmon, then the topping and season with pepper.

Smørrebrød for spring and summer

Smørrebrød is very seasonal, like Scandinavian food in general. In summer one of the all-time classics is rye bread with boiled potatoes, mayo and onion, capers or horseradish. Try it and create your own combinations. ALL SERVE 2.

Herring

2 slices of rye bread
150g white herring in brine,
    or rollmops
20 slices of red onion
6 sprigs of dill
salt and freshly ground
    pepper

Place the bread slices on a small serving board or plate. Place the pieces of marinated herring on top of them, followed by the onion slices and the dill. Season and serve right away.

Egg and tomato

2 tbsp cottage cheese
1 tsp Dijon mustard
salt and freshly ground
    pepper
2 slices of rye bread
20g rocket leaves
2 organic hard-boiled eggs,
    sliced
2 tomatoes, sliced
cress

Mix the cottage cheese and mustard with a pinch of salt and pepper.
Place the bread slices on a small serving board or plate. Put some rocket leaves on them, followed by the egg and tomato slices. Spoon 1 tablespoon of the cottage cheese mixture on top and sprinkle with salt and pepper. Place the cress on top and serve right away.

Potatoes

2 slices of rye bread
200g boiled new potatoes,
    sliced
1 tbsp chopped spring onion

horseradish cream
2 tbsp Greek yoghurt (10% fat)
1 tbsp grated fresh
    horseradish, plus more
    to serve
½ tsp sugar
1 tbsp lemon juice
salt and freshly ground
    pepper

Make the horseradish cream by mixing all the ingredients. Place the bread slices on a small serving board or plate. Arrange the potato slices on them, place a tablespoon of the cream on top and then sprinkle with spring onion and salt and pepper. Place some horseradish on top of the cream. Serve right away.

Spinach and duck salad
with horseradish dressing

2 duck legs or other leftover
  duck meat
1 bay leaf
2 cloves
salt and freshly ground
  pepper

salad
200g baby spinach
50g walnuts
2 pears, sliced

horseradish dressing
100ml non-fat yoghurt
2-3 tbsp freshly grated
  horseradish
½ tsp sugar
1-2 tbsp lemon juice

SERVES 4

TIP You can also use leftover
chicken, turkey, or lamb in place of
the duck - about 300g.

**Both winter or summer spinach will work for this salad,
perfect for any kind of leftover meat or poultry. If you don't
eat meat, replace the duck with baked root vegetables.**

In a cast iron pot or similar over a high heat, brown the duck
legs all over, in their own fat. When golden brown, season with
salt and pepper, add the bay leaf, cloves and just a little water
to a depth of about 1–2cm. Let it simmer until the duck is done
– about 1 hour. Check them regularly; when they are done, the
meat should fall from the bone. Set aside to cool.

For the salad, rinse the spinach in cold water. Drain and set
aside in a colander.

For the horseradish dressing, mix together all the
ingredients.

When the duck legs are ready, cut them into slices or tear
into strips. Toast the walnuts in a dry pan, then roughly chop.
Mix the spinach, duck, pears and walnuts together in a bowl
and, just before serving, fold in the dressing. Season to taste
with salt and pepper.

Prawn salad

200g green beans
1 small head of romaine salad
1 tsp fennel seeds
2 tsp butter
2 slices of rye bread, cut into
  small cubes
300g cooked small prawns
  or shrimps
4 tbsp dill, roughly chopped
2 tbsp fresh tarragon,
  roughly chopped
2 tbsp lemon juice
2 tbsp extra virgin olive oil
salt and freshly ground
  pepper

SERVES 4

TIP You could also use steamed
or baked leftover fish in place of
the prawns.

In the Nordic countries we eat very seasonally, not only
when it comes to ingredients, but also according to the
weather. I love to eat salads both for lunch and dinner,
and in the summer I eat a lot of green salad, because that
is when it tastes best, and it is particularly perfect for hot
summer days.

Cut up the beans into shorter lengths, then boil them in salted
water for 3–5 minutes. When they are done, take them out of
the water and rinse them in cold water. Drain in a colander
and set aside.

Rinse the salad leaves and chop them. Toast the fennel
seeds in a dry pan for a few minutes, then remove from the
pan and set aside to cool. Put the butter in the same pan
and toast the rye bread until crisp, then leave to cool.

Put the prawns in a big bowl with all the remaining
ingredients and season to taste with salt and pepper.

Nordic taramasalata
with rye bread

400g cod's roe

1 spring onion, chopped

2 tbsp each chopped dill
   and chives

2 tbsp extra virgin rapeseed
   or olive oil

3 tbsp lemon juice or
   to taste

brine

1 tbsp coarse sea salt

1 tbsp whole black
   peppercorns

3 slices of unwaxed lemon

**SERVES 4 (OR 2 FOR
LUNCH FOR 2 DAYS)**

TIP If you make a portion and store
it in the fridge for your lunch box,
it will last for 3 days.

This is my Nordic version of taramasalata, using cod's roe.
If you can't get cod's roe, then you can use roe from other
local fish in season. Although fish eggs, like hens' eggs, are
high in cholesterol, they are an excellent source of vitamin
C and a very good source of protein.

First make the brine: pour 3 litres of water into a large pot and
add the brine ingredients. Bring to the boil, place the roe in
the brine and simmer for 30 minutes. Take the roe out of the
water with a slotted spoon and leave to cool.

Remove and discard the membrane from the roe, place in a
food processor with the other ingredients and blend until you
have an even paste. Take out of the food processor and season
with salt and pepper.

Serve with rye toast and a green salad, dressed with a little
lemon juice.

Green salad with radish, smoked mackerel or smoked herring

200g smoked mackerel
   or herring
400g boiled new potatoes,
   sliced
100g frisée leaves, torn
   into pieces
100g lamb's lettuce
10 radishes, sliced
4 tbsp chopped chives
150g small tomatoes,
   halved
rye bread, to serve

dressing
150ml low-fat natural
   yoghurt
2 tbsp Dijon mustard
2 tbsp lemon juice
salt and freshly ground
   pepper

SERVES 4

In summer I serve this salad for either dinner or lunch, as it is both filling and fresh, making the perfect light meal on a hot day.

Remove the skin and any bones from the smoked fish and divide the flesh into smaller pieces. Mix these and all the remaining salad ingredients in a serving bowl.

Make the dressing by mixing all the ingredients together. Serve the salad with rye bread and the dressing on the side.

RADISHES are among the oldest cultivated plants we have. They originate from China and the Egyptians grew radishes before the time of the pyramids. They are extremely easy to grow, developing in a very short time, and can therefore be sown several times during spring, summer and early autumn.

Spring salads

Serve these two salads together with a simple green salad for supper with home-baked bread. **BOTH SERVE 4.**

Asparagus salad

1 bunch of asparagus
2 lemons
2 tbsp pine nuts
1 tbsp extra virgin olive oil
salt and freshly ground pepper

Break off the lowest third of each asparagus stalk (save the ends for a vegetable stock or soup) and cut the stalks lengthwise into very thin slices.

Peel one whole lemon, removing all the bitter white pith under the skin. Cut out each segment of lemon flesh by cutting down in between the membranes and the flesh.

Toast the pine nuts in a dry pan until golden (this takes a couple of minutes and be careful not to let them burn).

Mix the asparagus, lemon segments and pine nuts together in a mixing bowl with the juice of the second lemon and the olive oil. Season to taste with salt and pepper.

Spring spelt pasta salad with parsley pesto

300g spelt pasta

parsley pesto
100g curly parsley, top leaves only
1 small garlic clove, chopped
3 tbsp extra virgin rapeseed oil or olive oil
40g almonds
3 tbsp lemon juice
salt and freshly ground pepper

Rinse the parsley in cold water and drain in a colander. Place in a food processor with the other ingredients except the salt and pepper, and blend to a smooth paste. Season to taste with salt and pepper and perhaps more lemon juice.

Boil the spelt pasta in lightly salted water for 8-10 minutes until al dente. Drain in a colander and allow it to cool down. When cool, place in a mixing bowl, mix with the pesto and season again with salt and pepper.

Smoked mackerel salad on rye bread

½ smoked mackerel
½ cucumber, thinly sliced
1 small red onion,
    finely chopped
1 bunch of chives,
    finely chopped
1 tbsp capers, rinsed
    and drained
1 hard-boiled egg,
    finely chopped
100g frisée leaves
salt and freshly ground
    pepper

to serve
2 slices of rye bread
5-6 radishes, chopped

SERVES 2

Smoked mackerel is best in August as the mackerel has by then become fully grown and is therefore a bit fattier, which makes it perfect to smoke. It can also be quite overpowering in its taste in August if just fried. Mackerel is one of the richest sources of omega-3 fatty acids, which are very important for our bodies.

Carefully remove and discard all bones and skin from the mackerel and break up the mackerel meat into small pieces.
    Mix the mackerel, cucumber, onion, chives, capers, egg and frisée leaves in a bowl. Season to taste with salt and pepper.
    Serve the mixture on rye bread, topped with the radishes.

Summer salads

That you can't get full on vegetables alone is a myth – it is just another kind of feeling where you can still move and don't have to lie down for half an hour after dinner to let your food be digested. What I want to emphasize is that you might need to get used to not eating meat every day; changing your diet from meat to a lot of vegetables will give you energy after meals, but it can take a few weeks to adjust. However, you will certainly soon feel the benefits. ALL SERVE 4.

Pointed cabbage with prawns, watercress and radish

200g pointed cabbage
200g cooked and peeled
    coldwater prawns
150g radishes, sliced
50g watercress
2 tbsp white wine vinegar
1 tbsp extra virgin olive oil
salt and freshly ground
    pepper

Cut the cabbage into slices, rinse in cold water and drain in a colander.
    In a mixing bowl, mix the cabbage, prawns, radishes, watercress, vinegar and oil. Season to taste with salt and pepper. Serve right away.

Tomato and cucumber with fresh mint

1 cucumber
250g red and yellow cherry
    tomatoes (or big ones)
2 tbsp chopped mint
salt and freshly ground
    pepper
juice from ½ lemon
2 tbsp extra virgin olive oil

Cut the cucumber in half lengthwise and scrape out the seeds, then cut in slices. Cut the tomatoes in half. In a serving bowl, mix the cucumber, tomatoes, mint, lemon juice and olive oil. Season to taste with salt and pepper, and serve.

Fennel with strawberries, goat feta and vinaigrette

1 head of fennel
150g strawberries, sliced
125g crumbled goat feta

dressing
50g raspberries
2 tbsp raspberry vinegar

Cut the fennel in super-thin slices on a mandoline grater, then place in a bowl of cold water. Leave for half an hour. Drain in a colander.
    Mix the strawberries, fennel and goat feta.
    Make the dressing: add the raspberries and raspberry vinegar to a blender and blend until well mixed. Toss the salad with the dressing and serve right away.

Autumn salads

In autumn you'll find plenty of root vegetables, which you can use for a lot of different salads. Basically they can all be baked and served with a yoghurt or oil and vinegar dressing, Most root vegetables can also be eaten raw, although they often need to be thinly sliced or grated otherwise they are too hard to chew. ALL SERVE 4.

Jerusalem artichoke with cold sauce verte

600g Jerusalem artichoke

sauce verte
100ml low-fat yoghurt
3 tbsp chopped dill
3 tbsp chopped parsley
1-2 tsp lemon juice
salt and freshly ground
    pepper

Mix all the ingredients for the sauce verte in a large mixing bowl.

Peel the Jerusalem artichokes and cut into very thin slices, adding them directly to the sauce verte to make sure they do not discolour. Season to taste with salt and pepper.

Blueberries and blue cheese

150g fresh spinach leaves
150g blueberries or any berry
    or fruit in season
75g blue cheese, cut into
    small cubes

dressing
2-3 tbsp balsamic vinegar
1 tbsp extra virgin olive oil
salt and freshly ground
    pepper

Rinse the spinach in plenty of cold water 3 or 4 times. Drain in a colander. Rinse the blueberries and drain well.

Place the spinach in a big bowl and mix in the blueberries and blue cheese. Whisk the dressing ingredients together and mix in with the salad. Season to taste with salt and pepper.

Raw red cabbage

50g walnuts
200g red cabbage, finely
    shredded
1 apple, thinly sliced

dressing
1 tsp apple jelly
1½ tbsp white wine vinegar
1 tbsp walnut oil
salt and freshly ground
    pepper

Toast the walnuts carefully in a dry pan until golden, then chop them roughly.

Mix the red cabbage, apples and walnuts in a serving bowl.

Make the dressing by whisking together the apple jelly and vinegar, then whisk in the oil. Season to taste with salt and pepper. Mix into the cabbage salad and serve.

Kale and chicken salad

1 organic chicken
1 tbsp salt
1 tbsp whole peppercorns
2 bay leaves
300g celeriac
300g raw kale
Country Bread (page 168),
   to serve

dressing
2-3 tbsp Dijon mustard
3 tbsp lemon juice
1 tbsp extra virgin olive oil
1 tbsp chopped capers

SERVES 4

Kale is a winter superfood; use it for salad in place of lettuce, in pasta dishes and add to mashed potatoes – think of your own ways to use kale in your everyday winter food.

Gently boil the chicken in 3 litres of water with the salt, peppercorns and bay leaves for an hour or until cooked through. Leave to cool in the stock.

Preheat the oven to 200ºC/gas mark 6. Peel the celeriac and cut it into sticks. Place these in a ovenproof dish and sprinkle with salt and pepper. Bake in the preheated oven for 20 minutes and allow these to cool down as well.

Take the chicken out of the stock and save the stock for soup or risotto. Skin the chicken and remove the flesh from the bones.

Chop the kale finely and mix with the chicken and celeriac in a serving bowl.

Make the dressing by mixing the mustard and lemon juice, then slowly add the oil and the capers. Mix into the salad and season to taste with salt and pepper.

Serve with Trine's Country Bread.

KALE is a fantastic source of soluble fibre and a lot of vitamins. It is easy to grow, particularly in colder temperatures, where a light frost will produce especially sweet leaves.

Winter salads

You can make tasty salads all year round; simply combine winter vegetables in all kinds of ways, and mix them with different dressings. Serve the following three salads together as supper with Spelt Bread (page 171). ALL SERVE 4.

Potato and kale

400g potatoes
500g kale

dressing
2 tbsp grainy mustard
2 tbsp hot mustard
1 tsp honey
1 tbsp grated horseradish
1 tbsp diced shallots
1 tbsp white wine vinegar
2 tbsp extra virgin olive oil
salt and freshly ground
    pepper

Peel the potatoes if needed, boil until tender, then cut into chunks. Cut the stalks from the kale and chop the leaves finely. Mix with the potatoes.
  Make the dressing by whisking the mustards, honey, horseradish, shallots and vinegar together. Still whisking, gradually add the oil. Season with salt and pepper and mix into the salad.

Brussels sprouts with apples and walnut oil

500g Brussels sprouts
salt and freshly ground
    pepper
200g apples, sliced
1 green chilli, deseeded and
    chopped
2 tbsp apple cider vinegar
2 tbsp walnut oil

If necessary discard the outer leaves of the sprouts, then cut the sprouts in half. Cook them in salted boiling water for 5 minutes, then drain.
  In a mixing bowl, mix the sprouts with the apple slices, chilli, vinegar and walnut oil, and season to taste with salt and pepper.

Scorzonera with red onion and parsley

500g scorzonera
milk, to soak
1 tbsp olive oil
1 red onion, halved and sliced
salt and freshly ground
    pepper
8 tbsp roughly chopped
    flat-leaf parsley

Peel the scorzonera and rinse in water, then cut into thick slices and put to soak in milk to prevent discolouration.
  Fry the drained slices in the oil in a frying pan with the red onion for 3-5 minutes. Sprinkle with salt and pepper, transfer to a serving plate and sprinkle with the parsley.

Salads with grains

Grains are wonderful ingredients, full of flavour and texture, and very healthy – all qualities that make them perfect for salads. If you can't find the pearl version of barley, rye or spelt, use the whole variety and cook for longer, until tender. ALL SERVE 4.

Pearl barley with beetroot

100g pearl barley
2 red onions, cut into wedges
200g raw beetroot
a big bunch of dill, chopped
salt and freshly ground
   pepper

dressing
2 tbsp raspberry vinegar
2 tbsp extra virgin olive oil

Rinse the barley in cold water, then boil in salted water for 15-20 minutes or until tender. Set aside to cool. Preheat the oven to 200ºC/gas mark 6.
   Place the onion wedges on baking paper in a roasting tin, sprinkle with salt and pepper, then bake in the oven for 10 minutes. Set aside to cool.
   Peel the beetroot and cut into very thin slices, then mix with the dill, barley and onions. Toss in the mixed dressing ingredients and season with salt and pepper.

Rye with tomatoes and courgette

100g pearl rye
1 courgette, cut into cubes
2 tbsp extra virgin olive oil
2 tbsp tarragon vine vinegar
1 small garlic clove, crushed
150g cherry tomatoes, halved
150g yellow cherry tomatoes, halved
2 tbsp chopped mint
2 tbsp chopped tarragon

Rinse the rye in cold water, then boil in salted water for 15-20 minutes or until tender. Set aside to cool.
   Fry the courgette cubes in the oil until golden brown, then turn off the heat and add the vinegar and garlic. Set aside to cool.
   Mix together all the ingredients, season to taste with salt and pepper, and if it's too dry, add a bit more olive oil.

Pearl spelt

100g pearl spelt
200g green beans
4-6 tbsp chopped chives
10 radishes, cut lengthways
1 small head of romaine
   lettuce, chopped
a big bunch of flat-leaf
   parsley, chopped
salt and freshly ground
   pepper

dressing
1 tsp honey
1 tbsp Dijon mustard
2 tbsp white vine vinegar
2 tbsp extra virgin olive oil

Rinse the spelt in cold water, then boil in salted water for 15-20 minutes or until tender. Set aside to cool. Cut the beans on the diagonal and blanch for 2 minutes. Mix the dressing ingredients.
   Mix all the ingredients together and toss in the dressing. Season with salt and pepper.

vegetarian

The old concept of a meal always having to consist of 'meat and two veg' is now well and truly buried and there is no nutritional requirement for us to eat meat or fish every day, as most of us actually get too much protein. For a healthy, balanced diet it is a good idea to have at least two vegetarian meals during the week, as they are full of fibre and all sorts of nutritional goodies. There are many days during the week where I prepare a nice big salad, a vegetarian stew or pasta with vegetables. The important thing is that it has to be gastronomically interesting; it has to contain lots of flavours and texture. So use your imagination and experiment with all the wonderful array of vegetables, herbs and spices.

Mashed potato with a mixed vegetable topping

400g celeriac, peeled and
    cut into cubes
400g potatoes, peeled and
    cut into large cubes
2 garlic cloves, chopped
1 tsp whole peppercorns
1 tbsp sea salt flakes
2 bay leaves
2 tbsp olive oil

mixed vegetable topping

1 tbsp rapeseed oil
1 garlic clove, chopped
200g raw beetroot, peeled
    and cut into very small
    cubes
2 celery stalks, finely chopped
2 leeks, finely chopped
50g walnuts, chopped
salt and freshly ground
    pepper

SERVES 4

This mash with sautéed leeks, celery, beetroot and walnuts is actually quite easy to prepare and makes a very tasty vegetarian dinner. It is one of my winter favourites.

To a large pot add the celeriac, potatoes, garlic, peppercorns, salt and bay leaves. Cover generously with water, bring to the boil and then let simmer for 30 minutes.

While the vegetables are cooking, prepare the topping: heat the oil in a sauté pan, add the garlic and beetroot and cook gently for 5 minutes. Add the rest of the vegetables and the walnuts. Continue cooking for 5 minutes more. Season to taste with salt and pepper. Keep the sauce warm.

Drain the vegetables and place in a big bowl, discarding the bay leaves. Add the rapeseed or olive oil and mash, mixing everything well together. Season to taste with salt and pepper.

Serve the mash in a bowl, topped with the mixed vegetables.

Spelt pasta with spring onions, asparagus, dill and peas

1 bunch of asparagus
400g spelt pasta
salt and freshly ground
    pepper
2 tbsp olive oil
2 garlic cloves, chopped
3 spring onions, cut into
    pieces
200g peas, shelled weight
4 tbsp chopped dill

SERVES 4

- -

TIP Here in the Nordic countries, we also eat our pasta with Parmesan or Grana Padano. I really love my vegetable pasta with a scattering of nice cheese on top. I really believe we should nurture inspirations we have received from other food cultures and I will never give up what I have learned from my European neighbours. We cannot – and should not – roll back time.

If you don't have much time to cook every day, it is a very healthy and easy solution to prepare pasta dishes with lots of vegetables and serve them with a green salad. I also believe that it is a myth that we should not have pasta for dietary reasons. Of course we shouldn't eat pasta portions the size of Mount Everest, but dishes with 75–100g of pasta per person are fine. Remember that the planet's population grew to over 6 billion people mainly on wheat and rice. Pasta also contains protein and the level of protein is even higher in spelt pasta.

Break off and discard the lowest third of the asparagus where it snaps naturally and cut the remaining stalk in half lengthwise.

Cook the pasta in salted boiling water, not stirring for the first 3 minutes as spelt pasta breaks easily, until al dente, about 8–10 minutes.

While the pasta is cooking, heat the olive oil in a sauté pan and add the garlic, asparagus, spring onions and peas. Cook gently for 5 minutes over a medium heat. Take care that the garlic does not burn.

Drain the cooked pasta; mix with the vegetables and season to taste with salt and pepper.

Serve right away, scattered with the dill.

DILL is an ancient medical herb even mentioned in the Bible. It's a myth that we use a lot in the Nordic countries, but we do use it for some classic dishes, most famously gravlax. Cooking it for too long ruins the taste, so always add it at the very last minute. It is very easy to grow, often self-sowing. The season is from June to late autumn.

Barley-otto

1 small butternut squash
3 tbsp olive oil
250g pearl barley
200g mushrooms
300g tomatoes
4 garlic cloves, finely
    chopped
1 shallot, finely chopped
1 sprig of sage
2 sprigs of rosemary
1 bay leaf
juice of 1 lemon
40g butter
salt and freshly ground
    pepper

SERVES 4

Grains can be eaten in many ways; this is lovely comfort food, very tasty and very filling. It is also a great way to use up leftover vegetables, as all vegetables can be used.

Preheat the oven to 180°C/gas mark 4.

Peel the butternut squash and cut the flesh into 1cm cubes. Place in a roasting tin and mix with 1 tbsp of the olive oil, and some salt and pepper. Bake in the oven for 10 minutes.

Meanwhile, rinse the barley in cold water until the water runs clear. Boil in plenty of salted water for 20-25 minutes or until tender. Drain and set aside.

Chop the mushrooms and tomatoes into chunks. Add the rest of the olive oil in a big sauté pan and sauté the garlic, shallot, sage, rosemary and bay leaf for 3-4 minutes. Add the mushrooms and tomatoes and sauté for 5 minutes.

Add the boiled barley, baked butternut squash, lemon juice, butter, and some salt and pepper. Stir and let it simmer for 5 minutes.

Serve with a green salad.

Rye pasta with kale and garlic

400g rye pasta
salt and freshly ground
    pepper
500g fresh kale
2 tbsp olive oil
2 garlic cloves, finely chopped
1 shallot, finely chopped
1 fresh green chilli, finely
    chopped
side salad, to serve

SERVES 4

TIP In summer, replace the kale
with broccoli.

Nowadays, rye or spelt pasta can be very good quality.
With kale, it makes a simple dish that is perfect during the
week. As an additional bonus, it only takes 20 minutes to
cook for dinner.

Cook the pasta in salted boiling water, not stirring for the
first 3 minutes as rye pasta breaks easily, until al dente, about
8-10 minutes.

Cut off and discard the tough stalks from the kale, roughly
chop the leaves and rinse well.

Heat the olive oil in a sauté pan, add the garlic, shallot and
chilli, and cook gently for 2 minutes.

Add the kale and continue to cook for 5 minutes. Season to
taste with salt and pepper.

Drain the cooked pasta and mix the kale mixture into it.
Serve right away with a side salad.

Beetroot 'burgers'
with barley salad

beetroot burgers

250g raw red beetroot, grated

250g raw yellow beetroot, grated

100ml oatmeal

3 eggs

1 shallot, very finely chopped

4 tbsp finely chopped dill

2 tbsp finely chopped thyme

2 tbsp finely chopped parsley

salt and freshly ground pepper

1 tbsp rapeseed oil, for frying

barley salad

200g barley

1 celery stalk, finely chopped

a big bunch of flat-leaf parsley

1 tbsp extra virgin rapeseed oil or olive oil

2 tbsp red wine vinegar

SERVES 4

- -

TIP The burgers can be made the day before and reheated.

Beetroot is in season from May to November, but tends to be smaller in the spring, and the autumn harvest keeps well through the winter. A good rule is to go for the smaller ones for tenderness, especially if planning to use them raw in salads, and avoid very large ones, which may have a woody core. Try to get them with their leaves, which are also highly nutritious.

Mix the ingredients for the burgers well in a bowl, and allow to rest in the refrigerator for 1 hour.

Prepare the barley for the salad: boil it in water with a little salt for 30 minutes. Drain and allow to cool down. Set aside.

Preheat the oven to 180°C/gas mark 4. Form flat cakes of the burger mixture with your hands. Heat the oil in a frying pan and fry the cakes until golden on both sides. Transfer them to an ovenproof dish and put in the oven for 20 minutes.

Make the salad: mix the barley with the celery, parsley, oil and red wine vinegar. Season to taste with salt and pepper.

Serve the beetroot cakes with the barley salad. It is also a great idea to serve the horseradish dressing on page 121 with this dish.

BARLEY was possibly the earliest grain crop that man cultivated and it is still one of the most widely grown grains all over the world, as it seems to thrive in a wide variety of soil types. Most of the crop, however, goes into animal feed and the brewing of beer. Pot barley, the complete grain, is rich in soluble dietary fibre, so helps lower blood cholesterol levels.

Rye pizza with potato, or courgette and tomato topping

25g yeast
300ml lukewarm water
300g wholegrain
    stoneground rye flour
150g Italian tipo 00 flour
    or plain flour
1 tsp salt
1½ tbsp olive oil

potato topping

800g potatoes, cut into
    very thin slices
5 sprigs of rosemary,
    stems removed
salt and freshly ground
    pepper

**courgette and tomato
topping**

2 courgettes, each about
    250g, sliced
500g small plum tomatoes,
    halved
300g ricotta
salt and freshly ground
    pepper

**MAKES 2 (35CM) PIZZAS
(SERVES 4)**

**Nordic pizza for me is like regular pizza, but just with some
wholegrain rye or spelt flour added to the base. Choose
either the potato topping or the courgette and tomato
topping to make 2 pizzas – enough for 4 people.**

Dissolve the yeast in the water in a big mixing bowl, then add
both flours and the salt. Mix to a dough, then knead well until
smooth. Cover the bowl with a towel and leave to rise for
2 hours at room temperature.

Preheat the oven to 220°C/gas mark 7.

Roll the dough out to 2 very thin, large squares, each about
35cm. Place on a lightly oiled baking tray, then brush the tops
with olive oil.

To make the potato topping, place the potato slices evenly
over the pizza dough, brush again with olive oil, scatter the
rosemary on the top of the potato and sprinkle with salt
and pepper.

To make the courgette and tomato topping, space the
courgette slices and tomato halves evenly out on the dough,
then spread out the ricotta. Sprinkle with salt and pepper.

Bake the pizzas for 20-25 minutes. Serve with a green salad.

Vegetable biksemad with poached egg

2 tbsp olive oil
1 onion, chopped
200g peeled, cooked
  beetroot, cut into cubes
600g cold, boiled potatoes,
  cut into cubes
2 carrots, cut into cubes
2 celery stalks, roughly
  chopped
salt and freshly ground
  pepper
4 large eggs (as fresh
  as possible)
about 6 tbsp vinegar
4 tbsp finely chopped chives,
  to serve

SERVES 4

TIP If you like Worcestershire sauce, add a couple of spoonfuls to the mix and serve with organic ketchup.

This is my version of 'biksemad', a traditional dish normally made using leftover meat and potatoes with onion and Worcestershire sauce. It is usually served with eggs fried sunny side up and tomato ketchup. I developed this recipe when I was a vegetarian for some years. Enjoy my biksemad; it is the best healthy hangover food in the world!

Heat the oil in a frying pan, then add the onion and beetroot. Cook gently over a medium heat for 5 minutes, then add the potatoes and carrots and continue cooking for 10 more minutes. Lastly add the celery with some salt and pepper, and cook for 5 minutes more, stirring often so the vegetables do not stick to the pan.

Poach the eggs just before serving: use a sauté pan deep enough to hold 7-8cm of water and big enough to accommodate all 4 eggs at once. Add the vinegar (3 tablespoons per litre of water) to the water and bring to the boil. Break each egg into a heatproof cup and carefully lower it into the water. Lower the heat and simmer for 4 minutes. Remove the eggs with a slotted spoon and serve on top of the biksemad, sprinkled with chives.

Swiss chard
and skyr tart

pastry

75g plain flour
175g wholegrain stoneground
   rye flour
1 tsp sea salt flakes
75g butter
125g skyr or quark
butter for greasing the
   pie dish

filling

500g Swiss chard
2 tbsp olive oil
4 spring onions, sliced
5 eggs
150g skyr or quark
200g cottage cheese
1 tbsp fresh thyme leaves
1 tsp sea salt flakes
freshly ground pepper

SERVES 4

The chard can easily be replaced with broccoli, a very healthy vegetable – and we have grown to think of it as our own here in the North. My great uncle grew broccoli in his garden and he called it asparagus cabbage.

First make the pastry: mix the flours and the salt together in a large bowl, then crumble the butter in with your hands. Mix in the skyr or quark and bring together as a dough. Knead the dough with your hands. If you have a food processor, place all the ingredients in it and blend until it becomes smooth dough.

Roll out the dough on a floured surface and butter a 28cm pie dish. Line the dish with the pastry and leave in the refrigerator to rest for 30 minutes

Preheat the oven to 180°C/gas mark 4.

Cover the dough with baking paper and add some dried beans or rice. Bake blind in the oven for 20 minutes.

While the pastry is baking, rinse the chard well and cut it into pieces. Heat 1 tbsp oil in a pan and sauté the chard for 5 minutes. Drain in a colander. Using the same pan, add the remaining oil and sauté the spring onions for 2–3 minutes over a medium heat. Add the chard and thyme, mix well and remove from the heat.

Beat the eggs in a large bowl, add the skyr or quark, cottage cheese, salt and pepper, then the chard mixture. Remove the beans or rice and the paper from the tart base. Pour the egg mix into the blind baked pastry case and bake again in the oven for 30 minutes.

Serve warm with a green salad.

Leek and goat feta
tart on rye pastry

pastry

75g plain flour

175 wholegrain stoneground
rye flour

1 tsp salt flakes

75g butter

125g skyr or quark

butter for greasing the
pie dish

filling

500g leeks, cut into slices

2 tbsp olive oil

2 garlic cloves, finely chopped

1 tbsp finely chopped
tarragon

1 tsp salt flakes

5 eggs

150g skyr or quark

150g goat feta cheese

salt and freshly ground
pepper

SERVES 4

TIP A slice of this tart makes a
perfect lunch to take to work. One
of the best ways to rinse leeks is
first to cut them in slices and then
put them in a bowl of cold water
and leave for 5 minutes. Lift out
of the water so the grit stays at the
bottom of the bowl. Sometimes you
need to do this twice.

The tart revolution started in the 1970s, and I believe
it was partly started in Denmark by the vegetarian
restaurant chain Cranks, which opened a café in the
centre of Copenhagen. I loved their savoury tarts with
all kinds of vegetables. I still cook a lot of tarts, but I make
a dough using quark and rye flour and I also use a low-fat
dairy product instead of cream.

First make the pastry: mix the flours and the salt together into
a bowl, then crumble the butter in with your hands. Mix in the
skyr or quark and bring together as a dough. Knead the dough
with your hands. If you have a food processor, place all the
ingredients in it and blend until it becomes smooth dough.
If the dough does not come together, add a little water.

Roll out the dough on a floured surface and butter a
28cm pie dish. Line the dish with the pastry and leave in
the refrigerator to rest for 30 minutes.

Preheat the oven to 180ºC/gas mark 4.

Cover the dough with baking paper and add some dried
beans or rice. Bake blind in the oven for 20 minutes.

While the pastry is baking, rinse the leeks well. Heat 1 tbsp
oil in a pan and sauté the leeks for about 5 minutes. Drain in a
colander. Using the same pan, add the remaining oil and sauté
the garlic and tarragon for a few minutes, then mix in the leeks
and remove the pan from the heat.

Beat the eggs in a mixing bowl and add the skyr or quark
and goat cheese, then mix in the leek mixture. Remove the
beans or rice and the paper from the tart base. Pour the
mixture into the blind baked pastry case and bake again
in the oven for 30 minutes.

Serve warm with a green salad.

Cauliflower gratin

1 head of cauliflower, about
   600g, cut into chunks
1 red onion, sliced
1 tbsp olive oil
1 tsp butter
2-3 tbsp breadcrumbs
4 eggs
200g skyr or quark
100g cottage cheese
1 tsp ground nutmeg
salt and freshly ground
   pepper

SERVES 4

Since my childhood, this has been one of my all-time
favourites. We often had meat-free days, mostly because
meat was expensive. I have changed it a bit now and made
it lighter, without the heavy white sauce. This is perfect for
dinner, and you can serve it with one of the grain salads on
page 77.

Steam the cauliflower in salted water for about 5 minutes.
Remove from the water right away and leave to cool.
   Preheat the oven to 200°C/gas mark 6.
   Fry the red onion in the olive oil until golden at the edges.
   Grease 4 small ramekins, or 1 big ovenproof dish, with the
butter and sprinkle with breadcrumbs.
   Separate the eggs. Mix the yolks with the skyr or quark,
cottage cheese and nutmeg. Fold into the cauliflower in a big
mixing bowl, then add the red onions and season with salt
and pepper. Whisk the egg whites lightly and fold into the
cauliflower mixture.
   Spoon the cauliflower mixture into the prepared ramekins
or dish and bake for about 30 minutes.

fish and shellfish

We must try to eat fish at least twice a week, because fish is so healthy and tastes wonderful. As well as being low in calories and saturated fats, and high in protein, it is rich in a wide range of vitamins and minerals. Oily fish, such as herring, mackerel, salmon and sardines, are also good sources of the crucial omega-3 fatty acids which keep our hearts and our brains healthy and are quite hard to come by in other foods. The Nordic region has, I believe, some of best fish in the world, but of course I would say that and I really think that all countries or areas near the sea have incredible local fish. We should only eat local fish that have not travelled too far and are available during their correct (non-breeding) season. It is also vital to try fish that may not be fashionable to eat, but have great potential.

Summer fish pie

1kg new potatoes
600g cod or other white fish
25g butter, plus extra for
   greasing the dish
1 tsp fennel seeds
1 shallot, chopped
1 fennel
2 celery sticks
500g summer cabbage
½–1 tsp black pepper
2 spring onions, chopped
4 tbsp olive oil, plus extra
   for brushing
salt

SERVES 4-6

**I love fish pie so much. In the summer I make one that is
very light in texture, which is perfect for dinner. It is full of
flavour from the fennel and black pepper. 'Velbekomme!',
as we say in Denmark before we start eating.**

Boil the potatoes in salted water until soft but still firm. How
long this takes will depend on how old the potatoes are, and
their size, so check them regularly. While they are boiling, cut
the fish into chunks, butter an ovenproof dish and place the
fish in it so it covers the bottom.

Preheat the oven to 200ºC/gas mark 6.

Grind the fennel seeds with a pestle and mortar. Melt the
butter in a frying pan, then gently fry the crushed seeds and
the shallot for a couple of minutes. Remove them from the
pan and scatter over the fish.

Chop the fennel, celery and cabbage and sauté in the same
pan you used for the fennel and shallot. Fry for 5 minutes, then
remove from the heat and leave to cool a little before placing
over the fish as well.

When the potatoes are done, pour out the water, add the
black pepper, spring onions and olive oil and mash very lightly
together. Season to taste with salt. Spread the mash over the
fish and brush the surface with a little olive oil. Bake the pie in
the oven for 20 minutes. Serve right away.

Fishcakes with baked
potatoes and asparagus

500g skinless, boneless
　　salmon (or pollack or cod)
1 tsp sea salt
50g porridge oats
2 tbsp flour
3 eggs
2 spring onions, finely
　　chopped
50g grated carrot
50g grated ginger
1 tsp ground coriander
1 tbsp grapeseed oil, for frying
20g butter, for frying

baked potatoes
and asparagus
600g small potatoes
2 tbsp olive oil
salt and freshly
　　ground pepper
1 bunch of green asparagus
1 unwaxed lemon, cut
　　into wedges

sauce
250ml yoghurt
6 tbsp finely chopped parsley
2 tbsp finely chopped
　　mint leaves
salt and freshly ground
　　pepper

SERVES 4

**Fishcakes are a big part of Nordic food tradition. They
are prepared in many different ways; restaurants even
have their 'signature' fishcakes, and fish shops sell a
wide variety of them. I cook all kinds of different fishcakes,
some with salmon, others with cod, haddock or pollack.
They are wonderful as everyday food for dinner, or cold
with rye bread for lunch.**

Well ahead, blend the salmon in a food processor. Place it in a
bowl, add the teaspoon of sea salt and stir well, then stir in the
remaining ingredients. Place the mixture in the refrigerator to
chill for 1 hour.

　　Preheat the oven to 200°C/gas mark 6. Prepare the
potatoes for baking: put them in an ovenproof dish, drizzle
with olive oil, sprinkle with salt and pepper, and mix well.
Bake in the oven for 30-40 minutes, until tender.

　　Put the asparagus and lemon pieces in another ovenproof
dish and sprinkle with a little salt and pepper. Bake them with
the potatoes for their last 8 minutes in the oven.

　　Using a spoon and your free hand, shape the salmon
mixture into balls, then pat gently into flattish rounds. Heat
the oil and butter in a frying pan and cook the fishcakes over
a medium heat for 5 minutes on each side.

　　Meanwhile, make the sauce by mixing the ingredients and
season to taste with salt and pepper.

　　Serve the fishcakes with the potatoes and asparagus,
with the sauce served separately.

Mussel and cod stew with vegetables and white wine

500g mussels
2 celery sticks, cut into slices
2 carrots, cut into chunks
2 leeks, well rinsed and
    cut across into slices
salt and freshly ground
    pepper
200ml white wine
500g skinless cod fillets,
    broken into small pieces
spelt bread, to serve

SERVES 4

This fish stew is tasty and easy to make. Once you've assembled everything, it takes just 10 minutes to cook it and for it to be ready to eat.

Scrub the mussels thoroughly and tug out any beards that may be hanging from the shells. Discard any broken or open mussels or those that refuse to close when the shell is tapped. Rinse the mussels in cold water a couple of times.

In a large sauté pan, place the celery, carrots and leeks, then sprinkle with salt and pepper. Place the mussels in between and on top of the vegetables. Pour the white wine over the fish and vegetables. Cover with a lid and bring to the boil, then turn down the heat and let it simmer for 5 minutes.

Remove the lid and place the cod in between the mussels, sprinkle with salt and pepper and let it simmer again for 5 minutes.

Serve from the sauté pan with spelt bread.

Fried mullet with gooseberries and potato salad

2 grey mullet fillets,
 each about 400g
150g red gooseberries
20g butter

potato salad
400g new potatoes
200ml low-fat yoghurt
2 tbsp Dijon mustard
4 tbsp chopped dill
2 tbsp chopped chives
2 tbsp capers
salt and freshly
 ground pepper
150g shelled peas

SERVES 4

TIP Late in the season you can use lingonberries in place of the gooseberries, but then add 50g of sugar as well. If you want to grill mullet, brush the fillets with oil on both sides and grill at medium heat for a couple of minutes, then sprinkle with salt and pepper.

Mullet is a perfect summer fish that is easy to grill because its flesh is nice and firm. It goes well with the tasty but sour gooseberries.

Start by making the potato salad: cook the new potatoes in salted boiling water, drain and then let them cool down.

In a mixing bowl, mix the yoghurt, mustard, dill, chives and capers well and season to taste with salt and pepper. Cut the cooled potatoes into chunks, add to the dressing together with the peas and mix in gently.

Cut the mullet fillets into pieces. Rinse the gooseberries and drain.

Melt the butter in a frying pan and fry the mullet fillets skin side down for 2 minutes, then turn the fillets over and add the gooseberries. Let fry for 5-7 minutes. Sprinkle with a little salt and pepper.

Serve right away with the potato salad.

GOOSEBERRIES grow wild, and are cultivated widely across northern Europe. Although the green ones with the fuzzy skins are the most familiar in Britain, there are many varieties in different colours – white, yellow and red – and often with smooth skins. Closely related to the blackcurrant and redcurrant, they also vary in their degree of sweetness; some are sweet enough to eat raw, but most need stewing with sugar.

Fish, fennel and light mash

1 head of fennel
600-700g turbot or
   cod fillets
knob of butter
salt and freshly ground
   pepper
1 tsp fennel seeds

light mash
600g unpeeled small
   potatoes, well scrubbed
1 tbsp extra virgin
   rapeseed oil
2 spring onions, chopped
2 sprigs of dill, to garnish

SERVES 4

In summer there are plenty of white fish in season. If you are in any doubt about which fish are sustainable and fine to eat, visit the WWF website which has a great, easy-to-read list. Or look for the MSC certification on the fish packaging.

Cook the potatoes in salted boiling water. When just tender, drain them and place them in a bowl. Cover and set aside. Using a mandoline grater, slice the fennel super-thinly. Put in cold water.

Prepare the fish by cutting it into squares and fry in butter for 3-4 minutes on each side, until tender. (Frying time depends on how big they are, so keep an eye on them.) Sprinkle with salt and pepper. Remove the fish from the pan when done and keep warm.

Add the fennel seeds and the well-drained fennel to the pan and sauté for 3-4 minutes. Sprinkle with salt and pepper while the fennel is cooking.

Mash the potatoes roughly with a big balloon whisk, then add the oil and the spring onions, salt and pepper. The mash should be very lumpy.

Serve the fish on top of the fennel, and add some fresh dill sprigs on top of the fish. Serve with the mash.

Salmon with carrots, ginger, leeks, green beans and chervil

4 pieces of salmon fillet,
    about 700-800g
200g baby carrots
1 leek, cut into fine
    julienne strips
200g green beans,
    trimmed of ends
100g ginger, finely
    chopped
a bunch of chervil
salt and freshly
    ground pepper

to serve
200g pearl spelt
4 tbsp chopped chives
6 tbsp chopped parsley
2 tbsp extra virgin olive oil
green salad

SERVES 4

Salmon is a very northern-hemisphere fish and we eat a lot of it in many different ways: raw, smoked, cold, fried, baked, marinated or as gravlax. Here I fry the fish in a dry pan, so it cooks in its own oils for a good, true flavour.

Boil the pearl spelt in salted water for about 20 minutes, or until cooked. Keep warm while you prepare the salmon.

Fry the salmon in a hot dry pan for 2-3 minutes on each side. Remove the salmon from the pan, add the vegetables, ginger and chervil, and let them cook for 5 minutes. Season to taste with salt and pepper.

Place the salmon fillets on a serving platter and spread the cooked vegetables over them. Mix the warm pearl spelt with the herbs and olive oil and season to taste with salt and pepper. Serve with the salmon and a green salad.

Fried mackerel with baked rhubarb and pointed cabbage

4 rhubarb stalks
50g raw organic sugar
light vegetable oil,
   for brushing
2 large whole mackerel,
   each about 700g
1 unwaxed lemon, sliced
1 pointed cabbage
20g butter
salt and freshly
   ground pepper

to serve
4 slices of spelt or rye bread

SERVES 4

TIP If you want your rhubarb a little sweeter add the sugar.

A very oily fish, mackerel is also very beautiful, with its characteristic black and dark green colouring. It can be caught all year round, but most commonly during spring and summer. In August it is perfect for smoking, as the fat content is at its highest then. I use rhubarb as a savoury ingredient that goes very well with fatty fish.

Preheat the oven to 180°C/gas mark 4 and a hot grill or griddle pan.
   Cut the rhubarb into pieces about 3cm thick and mix with the sugar. Place in an ovenproof dish and bake in the oven for 15 minutes.
   While the rhubarb is baking, brush the mackerel with a little oil and grill or griddle for 5-8 minutes on each side and grill the lemon slices for a couple of minutes on each side as well.
   Cut the cabbage lengthwise into 6 pieces and rinse in cold water. Drain them well.
   Heat the butter in a frying pan, and fry the cabbage on all sides until golden brown and nicely caramelized. Sprinkle with salt and pepper.
   Serve the mackerel with the lemon slices, baked rhubarb, pointed cabbage and some spelt or rye bread.

POINTED CABBAGE forms a bright green narrow, oblong head and is an early vegetable in season from May to August. It has a short development time and is easy to grow but you have to harvest it at the right time as it has a tendency to bolt. It has the same strongly beneficial nutritional qualities as other types of green cabbage.

Baked haddock with
a lemon gremolata

½ pointed cabbage,
  shredded
1 bunch of asparagus,
  cut into slices lengthwise
1 head of fennel, cut into
  thin slices
800g skinless boneless
  haddock fillets
juice from 1 lemon
salt and freshly ground
  pepper

gremolata
1 tbsp olive oil
1 shallot, finely chopped
1 tbsp grated unwaxed
  lemon zest
50g almonds, skin on,
  chopped

yoghurt sauce
150ml yoghurt
juice from ½ lemon
4 tbsp finely chopped parsley

**A lovely spring dinner; use whatever local white fish
you can get. If asparagus is out of season, you can use
cauliflower or broccoli instead.**

Preheat the oven to 180ºC/gas mark 4.

Start by making the gremolata: heat the oil in a frying pan
and add the shallot, lemon zest and almonds. Let these cook
gently for 2 minutes. Turn out on a dish and set aside.

Put the pointed cabbage, asparagus and fennel in an
ovenproof dish and mix well. Now place the haddock fillets
on top. Pour over the lemon juice and sprinkle with salt and
pepper. Spread the gremolata over the pieces of fish and bake
in the preheated oven for 10 minutes.

Mix the ingredients for the yoghurt sauce, seasoning to taste
with salt and pepper.

Serve the haddock straight from the dish, with the cold
yoghurt sauce.

Cod with cauliflower in mustard dressing and spelt spinach stew

200g spelt kernels
500g spinach
1 whole cod, about 1.25kg
1 onion, cut in half
3 bay leaves
1 tbsp whole peppercorns
1 tbsp sea salt
1 cauliflower, separated
   into florets
1 tbsp rapeseed oil
1 garlic clove, chopped
salt and freshly
   ground pepper

mustard dressing
3 tbsp grainy mustard
1 tbsp Dijon mustard
6 tbsp chopped parsley

SERVES 6

Do ask your fishmonger or supermarket to ensure that the cod you buy is from a sustainable source.

Boil the spelt in a generous amount of water for 15-20 minutes, drain and leave in the sieve. Rinse the spinach well in cold water, remove any tough stems and drain well.

Cut the cod into large pieces, place in a pan and add the onion, bay leaves, peppercorns and salt with just enough water to cover the cod. Bring to the boil. Once boiling, turn off the heat and leave for 10 minutes with the lid on.

Sauté the cauliflower in a dry pan for a couple of minutes; if it starts to stick to the pan add a little water. Season with salt and pepper.

Make the mustard cream by mixing the ingredients, season to taste and then mix it into the warm cauliflower.

Slowly heat the oil and garlic in another sauté pan and then add the spinach and cook until wilted. Add the cooked spelt and mix well. Season to taste with salt and pepper.

Take the cod out of the water and place on a serving dish. Serve with the spelt and the cauliflower in mustard dressing.

Fried herring with beetroot and horseradish sauce

8 herring fillets, each
about 150g
100g wholegrain stoneground
rye flour
30g butter
4 slices of rye bread, to serve

beetroot
400g beetroots
75ml Blueberry Cordial
(page 153)
75ml water
salt and freshly ground
pepper

horseradish dressing
200ml yoghurt
1 tsp honey
2 tsp lime juice
50g horseradish,
finely grated
2 tbsp capers

green salad
200g green salad leaves
juice from ½ lemon

SERVES 4

TIP If you can't get fresh herring,
use mackerel or mullet instead.

I love herring as they can be cooked in many different ways. This is a healthy everyday recipe, which is also inexpensive because fresh herrings are not a luxury fish.

First prepare the beetroots: peel them and cut them into cubes about 2 x 2cm. Place them in a saucepan with the blueberry cordial, the 75ml water, very little salt and some pepper. Bring to the boil, then cover with a lid and let simmer for 10 minutes. Remove the lid, increase the heat and, if necessary, fully reduce the juice to a glaze while stirring.

Cut off the little dorsal fin from each herring fillet and rinse. Mix the rye flour, salt and plenty of pepper. Press the fillets skin-side down in the flour, so they are completely covered, and then fold them over.

Fry in the butter for 4-5 minutes on each side or until golden-brown.

Mix all the ingredients for the horseradish dressing, seasoning to taste with salt, pepper and maybe more lime juice.

Serve the herring with the beetroot, horseradish dressing and green salad dressed with lemon juice.

HORSERADISH comes from south-eastern Europe and western Asia, but grows well in the northern European climate, so in many ways it's one of our truly spicy foods. The plant grows wild in many places in the countryside. It is perennial and can be harvested as long as the leaves are seen.

meat and poultry

Game has been part of our food culture for centuries, and probably for thousands of years before we actually farmed animals. Primitive man would hunt wild animals and cook them over an open fire. Today we eat far more farmed animals, and much more than our bodies really need. For reasons both of our health and the knock-on effect it has on climate change, we need to start cutting down on the amount of meat we eat. However, meat is still a tasty treat, an important source of protein and an essential part of a lot of classic and wonderful recipes. Therefore, when we plan our diet we should reduce overall meat consumption and also start including game in our food, as being mostly wild and more seasonal, there is less waste included in its production. Moreover, animals that live and eat in their natural habitat have leaner meat with a wider range of nutrients and little of the growth-promoting and medicinal additives found in reared meat.

Chicken with baked rhubarb and cucumber-radish salad

1 organic or free-range
    chicken, cut into 8 pieces
salt and freshly ground
    pepper
300g rhubarb
50g raw organic sugar

cucumber-radish salad
1 cucumber, deseeded
    and sliced
1 bunch of radishes, sliced

dressing
100ml goat-milk yoghurt
1 garlic clove, finely chopped
2 tbsp chopped mint

SERVES 4

Rhubarb and chicken make a perfect match and a very tasty spring dish when the rhubarb is in season. Rhubarb is also fantastic as a savoury vegetable.

Preheat the oven to 200ºC/gas mark 6. Put the chicken pieces in an ovenproof dish, sprinkle with salt and pepper and roast in the preheated oven for 30 minutes.

Cut the rhubarb into pieces and mix it with the sugar in a bowl.

Take the chicken dish out of the oven, place the rhubarb under the chicken, put it back in the oven and roast for a further 15 minutes.

Make the salad: mix the cucumber and radish slices in a bowl. Blend together the dressing ingredients and mix this into the salad. Season with salt and pepper.

Serve the chicken and rhubarb with the cucumber-radish salad and boiled potatoes.

Tarragon chicken with Jerusalem artichokes and kale and carrot salad

4 organic or free-range
  chicken breasts on
  the bone
50g almonds, chopped
8 tbsp chopped tarragon
½ tsp salt
600g Jerusalem artichokes
3 garlic cloves, halved
2 tbsp olive oil
salt and freshly ground
  pepper

kale salad
300g kale
3 carrots

dressing
1 tbsp Dijon mustard
2 tbsp apple cider vinegar
1 tbsp walnut oil

SERVES 4

- -

TIP The almonds can be replaced
with hazelnuts.

Tarragon is one of my favourite herbs. I use it with chicken, in salads and fishcakes, and in dressings. I grow tarragon in my front yard in a large pot, which I move to my kitchen window in winter.

Preheat the oven to 200°C/gas mark 6. Cut a pocket in the side of each chicken breast for the filling.

In a bowl, mix the almonds, tarragon and salt. Stuff this filling into the pockets you've made in the chicken.

Cut the Jerusalem artichokes into chunks and place in a big ovenproof dish with the garlic. Mix in the olive oil, salt and pepper. Place the chicken breasts on top of the Jerusalem artichokes and bake in the preheated oven for 25 minutes. To prepare the kale salad, remove the tough stems from the leaves and rinse the leaves in cold water. Drain in a colander and then chop finely. Cut the carrots into julienne strips and mix with the kale.

Whisk the dressing ingredients together and mix into the salad just before serving.

Serve the chicken breasts with the Jerusalem artichokes and the kale salad.

CARROTS are packed with antioxidants, as they are the richest food source of beta-carotene, which the body converts to vitamin A. This is even more readily available when the carrot is cooked. There are early and late varieties, so the season is from June for forced carrots, July to September for early outdoor-grown carrots, October and November for the main crop and December onwards for the late main crops. As they are easy to store, carrots are available all year round.

Braised pheasant, plums and kale mash

1 tbsp olive oil
2 pheasants, each cut into
    4 pieces
2 garlic cloves, chopped
1 onion, chopped
3 bay leaves
a big bunch of parsley,
    chopped
300ml white wine
500g plums, halved
    and stoned

mash

600g potatoes, cut
    into chunks
100g kale, chopped
1 tbsp rapeseed oil
salt and freshly ground
    pepper

SERVES 4

TIP If you prefer, you can replace
the pheasant with a whole duck or
4 duck legs. Adjust the roasting
time to 2-3 hours for a whole duck,
or 1-1 hour 30 minutes for duck legs.

Pheasants are tricky, as they can be very dull if overcooked. The meat is different every time I cook it, so my best advice is to look after it and take nothing for granted. Cooking is like everything else in life: the more you do it, the better you become at it. Fresh pheasant is the best and, when you get it right, it is food made in heaven, with lots of flavour, texture and tenderness. If you don't feel up to the challenge, this dish works equally well with duck, chicken and rabbit pieces.

Heat the oil in a pan and brown the pheasant all over. Add the garlic, onion, bay and parsley. Cook for 3 minutes. Add the wine, season and simmer for 15 minutes. Add the plums and simmer for 15 minutes more.

While the pheasant is cooking, boil the potatoes in salted boiling water for 20 minutes or until tender. For the last 5 minutes of cooking, add the chopped kale, then drain but save some of the vegetable water.

Place the potatoes and kale in a mixing bowl and use a balloon whisk to mash them. Add the oil and mix it in, then add a little of the reserved cooking water to the mash for a nice smooth finish. Season to taste.

Serve the pheasant with the cooked plums and the mash.

Quail with scorzonera and Savoy cabbage

4 quails
a big bunch of flat-leaf
    parsley
4 garlic cloves, halved
salt and freshly ground
    pepper
12 scorzonera
milk, to cover
1 Savoy cabbage
1 tbsp olive oil

mash
200g Hamburg parsley or
    parsnips, cut into chunks
200g carrots, cut into chunks
300g large potatoes, peeled
    and cut into chunks
2 tbsp extra virgin olive oil
salt and freshly ground
    pepper

SERVES 4

TIP Instead of Savoy cabbage, you
can use kale or broccoli. Instead of
quail you can use poussins.

**These tasty little birds are perfect for supper on a Saturday
night. One is enough for me, but some might think it is too
little meat. However, that is what we need to get used to –
less meat, more vegetables.**

Preheat the oven to 200°C/gas mark 6. Stuff the birds with
the parsley and garlic, sprinkle with salt and pepper, and
place in an ovenproof dish. Bake in the preheated oven
for 25 minutes.

Start making the mash: cook the Hamburg parsley or
parsnips, carrots and potatoes in salted boiling water for
20 minutes, or until tender.

Drain, reserving a little of the cooking water, and place these
vegetables in a mixing bowl. Mash the vegetables, add the
olive oil and a little bit of the vegetable water, season to taste
with salt and pepper, and keep warm.

Peel the scorzonera and cut into small pieces. Place in milk
until you have to use them. Cut the cabbage into thin slices.

Add the oil to a pan, then sauté the scorzonera and cabbage
until tender, about 6-7 minutes. Season with salt and pepper.

Serve the quail with this and the mash right away.

HAMBURG PARSLEY, or turnip-rooted parsley,
is closely related to parsley but has a root that
resembles a parsnip or white carrot. Harvest from
September until the frost comes, then store in a dry,
cold place.

Venison meatballs
with baked root veg

600g minced venison

2 eggs

100g oats

50g wholegrain stoneground
   rye flour

10 juniper berries, crushed

3 carrots

1 onion, finely chopped

salt and freshly ground
   pepper

1-2 tbsp butter for frying

lingonberry compote,
   to serve

mash

400g Hamburg parsley
   (see page 130)

400g parsnips

2 tbsp olive oil

1 tsp aniseed, lightly crushed

1 tbsp rapeseed oil, for frying

400g red cabbage

50g walnuts

2 tbsp raspberry vinegar

200ml yoghurt (1% fat)

SERVES 4-6

**Venison is well suited to meatballs. If you can't get venison,
you can make the meatballs with lamb, beef or turkey.**

Make the meatballs: in a bowl, mix together the venison, eggs,
oats, flour, juniper, one of the carrots, shredded, and the onion.
Season to taste and let the mixture rest in the refrigerator for
30 minutes.

To prepare the baked root vegetables, peel the Hamburg
parsley and parsnips, and cut them lengthwise, then place
them in an ovenproof dish, mix in the olive oil, aniseed, and
salt and pepper to taste.

Preheat the oven to 180°C/gas mark 4. Take the chilled
meat mixture out of the refrigerator and use a spoon
and your free hand to shape the meat mixture into about
24 small round balls.

Fry these in a very little oil in a frying pan until they are
golden brown on all sides. Place in an ovenproof dish and
finish in the preheated oven for 20 minutes, together with
the prepared root vegetables.

While these are in the oven, prepare the salad: cut the red
cabbage into very thin slices and the remaining carrots into
julienne strips, then mix the cabbage, carrots and walnuts.
In another bowl mix the vinegar and yoghurt, then add to
the salad and mix well. Season to taste with salt and pepper.

Serve the meatballs with the baked root vegetables, salad
and lingonberry compote.

Nordic stew

20g butter
600g venison (see recipe
   introduction), cut into
   2cm squares
2 tbsp plain flour
12 juniper berries, crushed
2 garlic cloves, chopped
3 bay leaves
5 sprigs of thyme
200g pearl onions, peeled
300ml red wine
300g mushrooms, chopped
3 carrots, cut into cubes
400g Hamburg parsley
   (see page 130), peeled and
   cut into cubes
salt and freshly ground
   pepper

to serve
600g potatoes, boiled
2 sprigs of flat-leaf parsley

SERVES 4

TIP If you can't get venison you
can use lamb instead, and cook
it for about 1 hour.

Venison stew is very tasty, but you need to be careful not to overcook it as the lean deer meat can get very dry and lose its full flavour. Use the shoulder or the rump from deer, roe deer or moose.

Heat the butter in a large saucepan and fry the venison, turning it regularly, for 5 minutes.

Mix in the flour and juniper berries. Add the garlic, bay leaves, thyme and onions. Stir well, add the wine, mushrooms, carrots and Hamburg parsley. Stir well again and let simmer for 20-25 minutes or until tender. The time it takes to get the meat just tender can vary a lot, so keep an eye on it, and take it off the heat when it is just right. Season to taste with salt and pepper.

Serve with the boiled potatoes, garnished with the parsley.

Lamb stew with fennel, fennel seeds, white wine and elderflower cordial

2 tbsp olive oil
1 kg lamb shoulder or leg
    meat, cut into cubes
3 garlic cloves, finely chopped
2 celery sticks, diced
1 tbsp fennel seeds
2 bay leaves
10 sprigs of tarragon
3 leeks, sliced
2 fennel bulbs, sliced
    1cm thick
50ml elderflower cordial
500ml white wine
salt and freshly ground
    pepper

to serve
300g pearl barley
2 tbsp fresh tarragon leaves

SERVES 6

Here is another real summer dish – lamb with elderflower and fennel. Light and tasty, serve it with new potatoes or some boiled barley or spelt. Sometimes, instead of fennel, I just use summer cabbage, which also works really well.

Heat the oil in a big sauté pan and brown the lamb on all sides. Do this in batches, if necessary, to make sure the meat browns evenly all over and doesn't just cook slowly.

Add the garlic, celery, fennel seeds, bay leaves and tarragon to the pan with the lamb and mix well. Add two-thirds of both the leeks and fennel, reserving the rest for later. Sauté for a few minutes, then pour in the elderflower cordial and white wine, season with salt and pepper, stir well and bring to the boil. Skim any froth that rises to the surface, then turn down the heat and let it simmer for 45–55 minutes or until the lamb is tender.

Now add the remaining leeks and fennel and simmer for a further 5 minutes. Season to taste with salt and pepper.

Cook the barley in salted boiling water for 20 minutes and time it so it's ready when the lamb is ready.

Sprinkle the fresh tarragon leaves over the lamb before serving with the barley.

Pork chops with apple and celeriac

2 yellow onions
2 carrots
4 pork chops
1 tsp butter
10 sprigs of thyme
salt and freshly ground
   pepper

apple and celeriac salad
100g pearl rye
1 apple
200g celeriac
4 tbsp chopped mint
4 tbsp yoghurt
2-3 tbsp apple cider vinegar

SERVES 4

Pork is part of the staple diet in Nordic countries. The sweet taste of the meat works really well with root vegetables, and for me thyme and pork are a match made in heaven. This is a traditional dish made lighter and without the gravy.

For the salad, rinse the pearl rye in cold water, then boil in salted water for 20-30 minutes until tender. When done, rinse in cold water, and drain in a colander.

Cut the apple into thin slices. Peel the celeriac and cut into super thin slices. Mix all the salad ingredients together and season with salt and pepper.

Peel the onions and carrots and cut the onion in half. Season the pork chops with salt and pepper. Pan-fry them in the butter with the onions, carrots and thyme, turning the chops over now and then. The total frying time should be about 10-15 minutes depending on how thick they are.

Serve the chops and vegetables with the apple and celeriac salad.

desserts
and drinks

In our increasingly busy lives, there has to be a time
and a place for sweet and comforting food. I believe that
homemade cakes are the best because, again, you control
what is in what you eat. A lot of the chocolate bars and
biscuits, etc. that we buy are full of additives and high in
calories. If you buy chocolate, stick to good-quality dark
chocolate as you can't eat too much of it.

Yoghurt panna cotta
with redcurrants

400ml Greek yoghurt
  (10% fat)
100ml double cream
3 tbsp honey, plus extra
  to serve
3 gelatine leaves, immersed
  in cold water for about
  5 minutes
200g redcurrants

SERVES 4

- -

TIP You can make these the day
before; they make a very nice
dessert to serve at brunch.

Desserts do generally contain a lot of calories... that is
just the way it is, so don't eat them regularly, and certainly
not while trying to lose weight. However, these yoghurt
panna cottas are low in calories. Most puddings and cakes
unfortunately don't lend themselves to the making of
**low-calorie versions without ruining the result, so eat
fresh fruit instead.**

Mix the yoghurt, cream and honey well in a bowl.
   Lift the gelatine out of the water and heat it gently in a
small saucepan. Let it rest for 2 minutes, then slowly pour the
gelatine into the yoghurt mixture. Add half the redcurrants
and mix them in.
   Pour into 4 serving glasses and set aside until the yoghurt
starts to set, then put in the refrigerator to set for 4 hours
before serving.
   Serve cold with more honey and the remaining fruit on top.

Raspberry lime sorbet

450ml water
200g sugar
500g fresh or defrosted
   frozen raspberries, plus
   extra to serve
juice from 1 lime
mint leaves, to decorate

SERVES 4

This sorbet is both palate cleansing and refreshing to eat – and also very easy to make. By making it yourself you can control the sugar content. Try experimenting to see how low you can go on the sugar and still love it!

Mix just 250ml of the water and the sugar in a pot, bring to the boil, lower the heat and let it simmer for 3 minutes. Then chill this syrup.

Rinse the raspberries, dry them well and then press them through a sieve so you have a raspberry purée without seeds.

Mix the raspberry purée with the syrup, the remaining 200ml water and the lime juice. Taste to see if you need to add any more lime juice. Place in a plastic container and put in the freezer. Take it out 4 or 5 times every 15 minutes and stir thoroughly, then let it re-freeze. Alternatively, use an ice cream machine and, when finished, keep it in the freezer until you serve it, decorated with extra raspberries and mint leaves.

RASPBERRIES are members of the rose family and come in many colours apart from red: there are also black, purple, white, orange and gold raspberries. They both grow wild, and are cultivated, in the cooler parts of the world mostly of the northern hemisphere.

Rhubarb soup with yoghurt ice cream

700g rhubarb
2 angelica stalks
1 vanilla pod
220–250g sugar

baked rhubarb
2 rhubarb stalks, cut into
   1cm pieces
50g raw organic sugar

yoghurt ice cream
400ml low-fat yoghurt
50g homemade vanilla sugar
200ml double cream

SERVES 4

TIP If you don't have angelica you
need to use about 100g more sugar.

This cold soup is perfe:t for a warm, early summer's day.
Avoid bought vanilla sugar, which is usually just a chemical
cocktail; instead rinse a used vanilla pod and let it dry until
stiff, then put it in a jar of sugar for a few days.

At least 8 hours ahead, make the ice cream: beat the yoghurt
and sugar together until the sugar is dissolved. Whip the
double cream until it forms soft peaks and fold it into the
yoghurt. Freeze in an ice cream machine. If you don't have an
ice cream machine, pour it into a bowl and put it in the freezer
for at least 6 hours, but stir it 2 or 3 times during that time.

Make the soup: cut the rhubarb and the angelica into 2cm
pieces and place in a saucepan. Add water to cover. Split the
vanilla pod lengthwise and scrape out the seeds with a tip of
a knife. Add these and the whole vanilla pod to the rhubarb.
Bring to the boil, turn down the heat and let simmer for
30 minutes. It is important that you do not stir it at all,
otherwise the rhubarb will break up.

Line a strainer with muslin and strain the cooked rhubarb
through it. Return the strained liquid to a clean saucepan.
Add the sugar and let it boil, stirring so that the sugar
dissolves. Pour into a bowl and let it cool down.

When it has cooled right down, cover it and place it in
the refrigerator until ice cold.

Make the baked rhubarb: preheat the oven to 150°C/gas
mark 2. Place the rhubarb stalks in an ovenproof dish and
sprinkle the sugar over it. Bake in the preheated oven for
30 minutes. Take out and allow to cool down.

Serve the cold soup with the rhubarb and the ice cream
in the middle.

Apple and pear crumble
with oats and cinnamon

3 pears (about 400g)
3 apples (about 800g)
100g oats
100g spelt flakes
100g soft brown sugar
100g almonds, coarsely
  chopped
1 tsp ground cinnamon
150g butter, plus extra
  to grease
400ml Greek yoghurt,
  to serve

SERVES 8-10

....

TIP You can replace the apples
and pears with plums or any fruit
in season.

In autumn I make this afternoon cake that is perfect with
tea. I am sure that it is pretty healthy as there is very little
sugar in it, and it contains both fibre and heaps of vitamins.
When I serve it with yoghurt instead of whipping cream, it
is because I don't really care for whipping cream – I have
always preferred yoghurt or low-fat crème fraîche to cream.
Try it, it is very refreshing!

Preheat the oven to 200°C/gas mark 6.
    Cut the apples and pears in chunks, keeping the peel on
but discarding the cores. Butter an ovenproof dish about 30 x
40cm with straight sides. Place the fruit in the prepared dish.
    In a mixing bowl, mix the oats, sugar, almonds and
cinnamon. Divide this mixture evenly over the fruit and then
place small dots of butter all over the top. Bake for 30 minutes.
    Serve warm with Greek yoghurt.

APPLES originate from central Asia, but are now
grown worldwide. The fruits mature in autumn. There
are literally hundreds of varieties and their nutritional
profile does vary wildly from one variety to another.
They have a low glycaemic index so their use as a
snack keeps hunger under control for longer than
is the case with most other fruits.

Rhubarb and strawberry tart

500g rhubarb, cut into
   1cm pieces
1 vanilla pod
150g caster sugar
500g strawberries, halved
   or quartered
200ml crème fraîche or
   yoghurt, to serve

pastry
150g plain flour
125g wholegrain spelt flour
1 tbsp caster sugar
100g cold butter, cut into
   small cubes
1 egg yolk
100g skyr or quark

SERVES 8-10

It is not always necessary to use a lot of sugar and fat to make a tasty dessert. Sometimes the natural flavours of the ingredients are sufficient. Skyr is an Icelandic cultured dairy product, rather like a soft cheese, that is high in protein and low in fat. It is suitable for breakfast, salad dressings and desserts, or anywhere one would use yoghurt. It is said to have been used by the Vikings, but is currently unique to Icelandic cuisine.

Make the pastry: sift the flours and sugar into a large bowl. Add the butter and rub in until the mixture resembles dry crumbs. Make a hollow in the middle and add the skyr or quark and egg yolk. Gather the dough with your hands to form a soft but not sticky ball. Wrap in cling film and put in the refrigerator for 30 minutes.

Preheat the oven to 180ºC/gas mark 4 and lightly butter a 28cm round tart tin. Lightly flour the work surface and roll the dough into a round at least 35cm in diameter. Use to line the tart tin and trim the edges by rolling the pin over the top of the tin, pressing down to cut off the excess dough.

Cover the dough with a circle of baking paper and weight with dried beans or rice. Bake blind for 15 minutes, then remove the paper, etc. Bake for a further 15-20 minutes until light brown and crisp. Cool on a wire rack.

Meanwhile, put the rhubarb in a pan. Split the vanilla pod lengthwise, scrape out the seeds and mix with the rhubarb, then sprinkle with the sugar. Bring to the boil, cover and simmer very gently for 20 minutes without stirring. Allow to cool. Spread the rhubarb in the tart case and cover with the strawberries. Serve with crème fraîche or yoghurt.

Fruit cordials

I make cordial out of many types of berry. The uses for cordials are innumerable: in dressings instead of honey; added to the water when boiling root vegetables to give them sweetness; mixed with sparkling water to make fizzy drinks, which are much healthier than conventional ones as they contain less sugar and additives; poured over vanilla ice cream; diluted with water and frozen as ice lollies; added to champagne for kir royale; topped up with boiling water for hot drinks in winter. I use cordials for hot punch with rum or Cognac when I have a cold or a fever; this is way better than medicine. ALL MAKE 1–1.5 LITRES.

Elderberry cordial

1kg elderberries
500ml water
3 Bramley apples, quartered
500g sugar

Rinse the berries and leave on the stalks, but remove the coarse stalks. Put the berries, apples and the 500ml water in a pot, bring to the boil and simmer until the berries burst.

Line a sieve with muslin and strain the cooked berries and apples through it. Put the resulting juice into a clean pot and bring to the boil. Add the sugar and boil for 2–3 minutes, skimming any scum from the surface. Pour the hot liquid into sterilized bottles. Once opened, store in your refrigerator.

Blueberry cordial

1kg blueberries
500ml water
300g sugar

Rinse the berries and leave on the stalks, but remove the coarse stalks. Put the berries and the 500ml water in a pot, bring to the boil and simmer until the berries burst.

Line a sieve with muslin and strain the cooked berries through it.

Put the resulting blueberry juice into a clean pan and bring to the boil. Add the sugar and let boil for 2–3 minutes, skimming any scum from the surface.

Pour the hot liquid into sterilized bottles. Once opened, store in your refrigerator.

Redcurrant cordial

1 kg redcurrants
200ml water
350g sugar

Rinse the berries and leave on the stalks, but remove the coarse stalks. Put the berries and the 200ml water in a pot, bring to the boil and simmer until the berries burst.

Line a sieve with muslin and strain the cooked berries through it.

Put the resulting redcurrant juice into a clean pan and bring to a boil. Add the sugar and boil for 2–3 minutes, skimming any scum from the surface.

Pour the hot liquid into sterilized bottles. Once opened, store in your refrigerator.

breads

Homemade bread is one of the principal things that will help you when changing your diet. Factory-made bread is often full of sugar, salt and other additives. This is one of the reasons a lot of different diet movements have hit a chord by telling that us bread isn't healthy. Almost as important, though, is what industrial breads don't contain; only a small percentage use the whole grain with the germ, with all the fibre, nutrients and slow-release energy that these impart. On the other hand, homemade bread, using different kinds of wholegrain flours and without a lot of added fat and sugar, is health-giving and should be part of your daily diet. Not a whole loaf, mind you, but 1 or 2 slices a day. Baking your own bread gives you back control over what you eat, and it is not difficult at all if you build it into your routine. I spend about 2 hours a week making bread dough and baking; the rest of the time it takes care of itself.

Rye syrup bread

50g yeast
500ml lukewarm water
50ml grapeseed oil
100ml golden syrup
1 tsp salt
400g wholegrain
    stoneground rye flour
400g plain flour

MAKES 2 LOAVES

This is a soft bread with a sweet taste. It is perfect with cheese and in the mornings, either freshly baked or toasted.

In a large mixing bowl, dissolve the yeast in the 500ml water, then add the oil, syrup, salt and flours. Stir together then knead; the dough should be firm but a bit wet. Leave under a tea towel to rise for 45 minutes.

At the end of this time, divide the dough into 2 pieces and leave to rise again for 30 minutes, then place into 2 loaf tins.

Preheat the oven to 180°C/gas mark 4 and bake the loaves for 1 hour in the preheated oven.

Leave to cool on a wire rack.

Rye buns

50g fresh yeast
400ml water
200ml yoghurt
2 tbsp honey
500g wholegrain
   stoneground rye flour
200g plain flour
1 tbsp salt
1 egg, beaten, to glaze
poppy seeds, to sprinkle

MAKES 20 BUNS

TIP The buns will last for 3-4 days, and are also delicious when toasted. Remember never to store your bread in the fridge, as it will make the bread dry. Instead, store it in a dark, cool cupboard or breadbox.

Buns can be served for breakfast, lunch and tea, but this dough can also be made into a large loaf and baked for 40 minutes.

In a bowl, dissolve the yeast in the 400ml water and add the yoghurt and honey. Mix the rye flour, plain flour and salt, and stir into the yeast mixture for about 5 minutes. On a floured work surface, knead this dough well.

Place the dough back into the bowl, cover with a kitchen towel and leave to rise at room temperature for about 2 hours.

Preheat the oven to 200°C/gas mark 6 and line some baking trays with baking paper.

As the dough is a bit sticky, dust your hands with flour and form about 20 small buns from the dough with your hands. Place the buns on baking trays lined with baking paper. Glaze the buns with beaten egg and sprinkle with poppy seeds.

Bake the buns in the preheated oven for 30 minutes. When they are done, let them cool on a wire rack.

Shower buns

10g fresh yeast
800ml cold water
10g salt
250g plain flour
550g spelt flour

MAKES 14-16 BUNS

TIP If you have time, leave the buns to rise for 20 minutes before baking.

This recipe allows you to have homemade buns for breakfast during the week without any hassle! The biggest bonus is that you get healthy, tasty, homemade bread! It takes no time at all to place the buns on a baking tray, put them in the oven, and they will be done when you come out of the shower. Not only do they taste wonderful, they will give your house that reassuring smell of home-baked bread in the morning.

The night before (or for at least 6 hours ahead): in a big bowl, mix the yeast in the 800ml water, then add the salt. Mix in the flours and give a good stir using a wooden spoon as it is a very soft dough. Cover the bowl with cling film and place in the refrigerator overnight.

Next morning: preheat the oven to 225ºC/gas mark 7 and cover a baking tray with baking paper. Take the dough out of the bowl and put it on a floured surface. Cut into as many portions as you want for breakfast and form into buns. Place on the baking tray and cut a cross on top of each with a sharp knife. (Put the remaining dough back in the fridge, covered.) Spray some water into the oven, then immediately put the tray of buns inside and bake for 25–30 minutes.

Take a shower while the buns are baking; they will be ready for breakfast when you are!

Let the buns rest on a wire rack for 5 minutes before serving for breakfast! Repeat every morning until there is no more dough left in the fridge.

Serve the buns with cheese, the rhubarb and strawberry jam on page 171, or a banana.

My rye bread

This is a rye bread that I eat every day either for breakfast or lunch. Sometimes, when I am very busy, I eat it for all my meals during the day. I also bring onto long-haul flights! Once baked, let it rest overnight before slicing into it. **MAKES 1 LARGE LOAF.**

Step 1: sourdough culture

220g wholegrain
   stoneground rye flour
300ml buttermilk
1 tsp coarse sea salt

Mix the ingredients in a bowl.
   Cover with foil and leave for 2 days in a warm place (23-28ºC). When it starts to bubble and smell a bit sour, it's ready. (If it smells before it bubbles, you have to start over again.) Then you have a sourdough culture! (If the temperature is too low, the sourdough will not develop but go bad.)

Step 2: making the dough

750ml lukewarm water .
15g coarse sea salt
750g wholegrain
   stoneground rye flour

In a large bowl, dissolve the culture from step 1 in the 750ml water. Add the salt and the flours, and stir the dough with a wooden spoon. It should be very runny.
   Cover the bowl with a towel and set aside for 20-24 hours at room temperature.
   IMPORTANT: the first time you use your sourdough culture, you will use all of it; from then on you use just 3 tbsp of your sourdough that you've set aside in a small jar.

Step 3: making the bread

250ml lukewarm water
500g cracked whole rye
   kernels

Add the 250ml water and rye to the dough and mix really well with a wooden spoon.
   IMPORTANT: every time you make rye bread, take out 3 tbsp dough and put in a jar. This is the starter for your next rye bread. Store in the refrigerator for up to 8 weeks.
   Pour the dough into a 3-litre loaf tin. (If it is not non-stick, brush the inside with oil.) Cover the tin with a towel and rise for 6 hours, or until it reaches the edge of the tin.
   Preheat the oven to 175ºC/ gas mark 4. Bake the loaf for 1 hour 45 minutes. Take out of the tin immediately and cool on a rack. Store in a tea towel or plastic bag.

Crispbread

50g yeast
500ml lukewarm water
300g plain flour
300g wholegrain
   stoneground rye flour
1 tsp crushed caraway seeds
1 tsp salt
100ml olive oil

MAKES 10

Eat crispbread as part of a snack with smoked salmon, or for breakfast, or with a salad for lunch.

In a mixing bowl, dissolve the yeast in the 500ml water. Mix the flours with the caraway seeds and salt. Add the oil to the flour. With your hands, mix the oil into the flour, then add the yeast mixture and knead well on a floured surface.

Put the dough in a bowl, cover with a tea towel and leave to rise for 1 hour at room temperature.

Preheat the oven to 250°C/gas mark 9. Roll the dough out in a little rye flour to a very thin sheet. Cut out about 10 big round crispbreads and then cut out a small hole in the middle of each. Prick the crispbreads all over with a fork.

Place on baking trays and bake for 5-7 minutes, or until golden brown.

Let cool on a wire rack. Store in an airtight container to keep them crisp.

Rye bread with linseeds and sunflower seeds

This rye bread has more seeds in it and therefore more calories, but it is extra healthy.
MAKES 2 LOAVES.

Step 1: sourdough culture

10g yeast
100ml buttermilk
100ml (measure it by volume) wholemeal wheat flour

Dissolve the yeast in the buttermilk. Mix the flour in well. Cover with foil and leave for 2-3 days at room temperature.

Step 2: making the dough

750ml lukewarm water
1 tbsp salt
300g cracked whole rye kernels
75g wholegrain stoneground rye flour
100g linseeds (flax seeds)
375g wholemeal wheat flour

Dissolve the culture from step 1 in the 750ml water. Add the salt, whole rye, rye flour and linseeds. Stir well, add the wheat flour and stir again to a runny dough. Cover the bowl with a towel and set aside for 12-16 hours at room temperature.

Step 3: making the bread

250ml lukewarm water
450g wholegrain stoneground rye flour
100g sunflower seeds

Add the 250ml water and rye flour to the dough and stir well. Then take 100ml of the dough, put it in a glass container, sprinkle with coarse salt, cover with a lid and store in the refrigerator. You now have a starter for next time you make rye bread; it will keep for up to 8 weeks.
  Add the sunflower seeds to the remaining dough and pour into 2 greased loaf tins (which have a combined capacity of 2.5kg). Cover the tins with a towel and leave to rise at room temperature for 6 hours.
  Preheat the oven to 180ºC/ gas mark 4. Prick the dough with a knitting needle or fork and bake for 2 hours. Let cool on a rack.

Country Bread

25g yeast
800ml lukewarm water
500g plain flour
200g wholegrain
   stoneground spelt flour
75g spelt flakes
75g oat flakes
75 barley flakes
10g salt

MAKES 2 LOAVES

Baking is for me a way of relaxing. This is a great one to bake during the weekend; you can then freeze one bread and eat the other during the week. It works really well for sandwiches, toasted in the morning, or sliced to accompany a salad or soup.

In a large mixing bowl, dissolve the yeast in the 800ml water. Add the flours, flakes and salt. If using a mixer, let it run for about 10 minutes; if you are making it by hand, stir with a wooden spoon for about 5 minutes. The dough will be very wet. Now leave for about 5 minutes.

Using a spatula, knead the dough well on a floured surface – just gently turn it around in the flour. Place it in a big bowl, cover it tightly with cling film and leave to rise at room temperature for 2 hours.

Put the dough back on the floured surface and divide in 2. Fold each portion of dough and tighten it up to form 2 round, slightly flattened balls of dough. Place each one in a well floured baking basket and leave to rise for 30 minutes.

Preheat the oven to 250ºC/gas mark 8.

Cover 2 baking trays with baking paper. Tip out each loaf onto a lined baking tray and, with a razor blade or very sharp knife, slash a cross over the top. Spray some water in the hot over to create steam and immediately place the baking trays inside. Bake for 10 minutes, then turn the heat down to 220ºC/gas mark 7. Bake for a further 35 minutes.

Remove the bread from the oven and leave it to cool on a wire rack.

Spelt bread / Rhubarb and strawberry jam

spelt bread
30g yeast
500ml cold water
1 tbsp flaky sea salt
3 tbsp rapeseed oil,
    plus extra to grease
100g oats
500g spelt flour

rhubarb and strawberry jam
(makes about 600g)
1 whole vanilla pod
300g fresh or frozen organic
    strawberries
300g rhubarb, cut into
    small pieces
100g caster sugar

MAKES 1 LOAF

If you bake your own bread, why not make your own jam? Recipes for jam were more or less developed before the invention of the freezer and refrigerator, so all the berries had to be used when in season. To ensure that the jam lasted for the rest of the year, you had to conserve it with a lot of sugar, which you don't need to do when you can store the jam in a refrigerator. Jam can be fresher with little sugar; it then tends to have a truer taste of the fruit.

First make the jam: split the vanilla pod lengthwise and place in a pan with the strawberries, rhubarb and sugar. Bring to the boil and let boil for 15 minutes; if it dries out at any point, add a little water. Pour the hot jam into sterilized preserving jars and seal tightly. Store in the refrigerator.

Dissolve the yeast in the 500ml water, then add the salt and oil. Mix again, then add the oats and flour and mix well for about 5 minutes.

Grease a 24cm diameter round baking tin or a 2-litre loaf tin with a little oil. Pour the dough into the baking tin and leave to rise in the tin for 4 hours and keep at room temperature. Preheat the oven to 200°C/gas mark 6 and bake in the preheated oven for 1 hour. Leave to cool on a wire rack.

Serve the bread with the jam (there's no need for butter as both bread and jam are so tasty).

Blueberry buns

50g yeast
700ml lukewarm water
10g salt
1 tbsp honey
100g oats
300g wholemeal flour
400g plain flour
100g blueberries
100g coarsely chopped
    walnuts
100g coarsely chopped
    hazelnuts

MAKES ABOUT 20 BUNS

I use these sweet and nutty buns as 'power snacks' to take with me when I go walking in the early morning at weekends.

In a large mixing bowl, dissolve the yeast in the 700ml water, then add the salt and honey together.

In another bowl, mix the oats and the flours, stir into the yeast mixture together with the blueberries, walnuts and hazelnuts. Mix well with a wooden spoon. Knead the dough gently for a couple of minutes.

Cover with a tea towel and leave to rise for 1 hour. Form around 20 buns, place them on baking trays lined with baking paper, cover with towels and let rise again for 30 minutes in a warm place.

Meanwhile, preheat the oven to 200°C/gas mark 6. Glaze the loaves with water and bake in the preheated oven for 25-30 minutes. Leave to cool on a wire rack.

Index

Acknowledgements

Creating cookbooks is always hard work and relies on great teamwork, so I have many people to thank. First 1,000 TAK to Quadrille for a great collaboration. A special thanks to Céline Hughes and Katherine Keeble for producing another great book, and to Helen Lewis and Sarah Lavelle for believing in me. 1,000 TAK to the sales team, especially Margaux Durigon and Hillary Farley for their great support.

1,000 TAK to my agent, Heather Holden-Brown, for her encouragement and support. Also to Lars Ranek for the beautiful pictures.

Thanks to my fantastic kitchen team, Anna Sofie Rørth and Stig Jensen, for inspiring me and coming up with useful critical remarks. Thanks to my stepfather, Henrik Rodam, for foraging with me in the woods and teaching me how to garden! And to my mother, Hanne Rodam, for all her support.

Thanks to my husband, Niels Peter Hahnemann, for still loving my cooking and clearing up after me after long days in the kitchen. And to my children, Michala and Peter Emil, for being honest in the most loving way.

PUBLISHING DIRECTOR Sarah Lavelle
ART DIRECTOR Helen Lewis
SENIOR EDITOR Céline Hughes
PHOTOGRAPHER Lars Ranek
DESIGNER Katherine Keeble
PRODUCTION Emily Noto

First published in 2010 by Quadrille Publishing as *The Nordic Diet*

This revised edition published in 2016
Pentagon House
52-54 Southwark Street
London SE1 1UN
www.quadrille.co.uk

Quadrille is an imprint of Hardie Grant
www.hardiegrant.com.au

Text © 2010 and 2016 Trine Hahnemann
Photography © 2010, except for pages 21, 52, 57, 58, 76, 85, 98, 103, 137, 138 and 169 © 2016 Lars Ranek
Design & layout © 2016 Quadrille Publishing

Cataloguing-in-Publication Data: a catalogue record for this book is available from the British Library.

ISBN 978 1 84949 763 3

Printed in China